The Island University

The Island University

A History of Texas A&M University-Corpus Christi

Andrew F. Johnson

Robert Furgason, Callie Walker

CONTENTS ▌

To the Islanders

Acknowledgement

Several individuals were supportive in the effort to write and share this book. Dr. Robert Furgason, who served as President of TAMU-CC from 1990 to 2005, authored the forward to this book and provided a wealth of information. It has been an honor to meet him and discuss the history of the institution he once led. Ms. Callie Walker edited numerous drafts of the book and provided valuable insight from her experience at TAMU-CC. Her work has been diligent and is most appreciated. The Director of the Mary and Jeff Bell Library Special Collections and Archives, Ms. Lori Atkins, and her staff, were most helpful in providing background information as well as historical photographs featured in the book. Dr. Paul Orser, who prior to his retirement served in numerous roles at TAMU-CC including as a professor and Associate Vice President for Planning and Institutional Effectiveness, provided a friendly review of an earlier draft of the book. I appreciate his valuable insight he was gracious enough to share with me on the history of the university. Mr. Russell Wagner was very supportive of this project in his role as Executive Director of Alumni Relations at TAMU-CC. The staff of the Marketing and Communications Department at TAMU-CC took many of the photographs that are attributed to the university and presented in this book. Their work adds a rich visual appeal.

I sincerely appreciate the efforts of each person who assisted me with the writing of this book to share the story of the Island University. All errors are my own.

-The Author

Forward

Rarely do existing organizations originate as they are currently configured. Most go through several phases of development that often occur over decades. During these development stages, memories fade or cease to exist and the current observer may be totally unaware of the energies, dedication, and resources that many of the organization's pioneers committed to the early creation and development of the organization.

In this volume, Andrew Johnson has managed to capture the evolution of Texas A&M University-Corpus Christi from the time the campus area was primarily a fishing and camping place for local Native American inhabitants to its current vibrant existence as a bustling academic campus serving over 10,000 students in a wide variety of degree programs and research endeavors.

The end of World War II provided an opportunity for advocates to pursue aspirations of having a higher education presence in South Texas and particularly the Corpus Christi area. The closure of many former military operations created a ready-made physical presence for possible development. The abandoned buildings and other facilities, although lucrative from a superficial view, posed many fiscal and operational challenges in using them for a new modest operation. For the most part, the U.S. Government wanted to rid itself of the entire operating base, not just a building or two. Thus, initial attempts to form a college in Beeville, and at Cuddihy Field in Corpus Christi failed.

The Baptist General Convention of Texas (BGCT) was the leading force behind creating additional higher education institutions especially for South Texas. However, it was also involved in creating many other colleges in Texas from Wayland Baptist University in Plainview to East Texas Baptist University in Marshall with several notable institutions in between including Hardin-Simmons University in Abilene, Howard Payne University in Brownwood, and Mary Hardin-Baylor in Belton; and of course, its premier campus Baylor University. Thus, its resources were stretched far and didn't provide much backing for a new university in South Texas. Financial support had to be mainly created locally.

Then Guy Warren and Howard E. Butt (creator of the HEB grocery firm) entered the scene and helped underwrite local funding for the newly created University of Corpus Christi which existed until the early 1970's when the institution became State supported. Johnson in this volume captures the further evolution of the university through its existence as Texas A&I University-Corpus Christi, Corpus Christi State University and Texas A&M University-Corpus Christi. His publication not only describes the academic development of the university but also identifies many of those leaders who were instrumental in its growth and advancement. Carl Wrotenbery's book, "Baptist Island College – An Interpretive History of the University of the University of Corpus Christi, 1946-1970," provides many insights into the early history of the campus and its leaders.

I was privileged to have been chosen to lead the university during its beginnings as a campus of the Texas A&M University System which involved its evolution from an upper-level institution to one that incorporates all levels of student activity from freshman to doctoral students. By necessity, this period involved hiring substantial numbers of new faculty, constructing the facilities needed to offer many new courses and programs, and building many infrastructure elements needed to support the new students and faculty.

The reader should enjoy learning of the development of the campus from its modest beginnings on the site of a U.S. Navy's Radar Training facility to its current extensive student-oriented operations. Ironically, what was an abandoned Naval flight facility is now the headquarters of a U.S. Government FAA operation, the Lone Star Unmanned Aerial System Center of Excellence and Innovation, which is one of only two test sites that NASA is supporting nationally for testing and development of unmanned aircraft systems (drones). It's come a long way!

By Robert R. Furgason, Ph.D., P.E.
President Emeritus of Texas A&M University-Corpus Christi

Introduction

Early Image of Corpus Christi (Circa 1846)
Corpus Christi Public Library

Texas A&M University-Corpus Christi is a four-year, doctoral degree granting university with its primary campus in Corpus Christi, Texas. With almost 12,000 students, it serves as the educational hub for the Coastal Bend Region of South Texas. The university was originally founded in 1947 as a private Baptist-affiliated college and has undergone significant changes and several iterations in its 75-year history.[i]

In 1998, the former President of the University of Corpus Christi, Dr. Kenneth A. Maroney, praised then-President of Texas A&M University-Corpus Christi Robert Furgason for "recognizing immediately upon his arriving that there was a history here."[ii] Maroney was correct about the rich history and keen to recognize the value in understanding the past of the institutions which shape our lives. Indeed, these two presidents led two very different universities in terms of student body, name, and character. Both leaders served during important times of transformation and continued to work on behalf of the institution after their tenure as president had concluded. They shared a common goal for advancing education through an institution that was founded 75 years ago. This book tells of the story of the Island University.

The History of Ward Island

Ward Island is a 223-acre site bordered by Oso Bay to the South and East and Corpus Christi Bay to the North.[iii] The Island overlooks Corpus Christi Bay and today has a picturesque view of Downtown Corpus Christi to the Northwest. Ocean Drive traverses the northern side of the island and connects to Naval Air Station-Corpus Christi (NAS-Corpus Christi). The Cayo del Oso shallow marshlands extend from Ocean Drive around the southern end of Ward Island to its eastern edge.[iv][v]

Earlier in its history, the area now occupied by TAMU-CC was sporadically inhabited by nomadic Native Americans who subsisted on seafood.[vi] The first people of the area that would become known as Ward Island were the Karankawa.[vii] This group lived in the Texas Gulf Coast region from present-day Galveston, south to Corpus Christi. Their name is derived from their practice of raising and keeping dogs. In their native language, the name Karankawa means "dog-lover" and refers to several bands of coastal peoples who survived on hunting, fishing, and gathering.[viii] The male Karankawa have been described as particularly tall and the people wore tattoos as well as jewelry made of shells, beads, and deerskin. They dressed in breechcloths and used animal grease on their bodies to repel insects.[ix]

Areas inhabited by the Karankawa were later occupied by European explorers followed by Mexican and U.S. settlers. The natives were not willing to be subjugated to living in missions or under the control of explorers or settlers in the area. Beginning with an encounter with the Spanish expedition of Panfilo de Narvaez in Galveston in 1528, the Karankawa had intermittent contact with Europeans (French and Spanish) until the 1700s when the Spanish unsuccessfully aimed to place them into missions.[x] Encounters between the natives and Europeans more often led to violence than peaceful trade.[xi][xii]

Settlement brought about rapid declines among the native population with European diseases being particularly devastating. The European explorers, Mexicans, and later Texans all had superior weaponry to the Karankawa even though they were described as very capable with a bow and arrow.[xiii] This disparity in weaponry meant that in armed conflict the natives would suffer mass casualties. A series of conflicts with settlers, including those under Stephen F. Austin, resulted in large numbers of fatalities for the native peoples. The last conflict between the Spaniards, under Juan Nepomuceno Cortina Goseacochea, and the few remaining Karankawa occurred in 1858 near Rio Grande City in South Texas. This armed engagement resulted in the virtual extermination of these native peoples.[xiv][xv] A small number of remaining Karankawa incorporated themselves into the colonizer's society, moved south to Mexico, or joined with other native peoples.[xvi]

Few reminders or tributes to the Karankawa people remain today. As their campsites were not permanent settlements, only small artifacts have been found. Some burial sites have been identified and have been protected. The Calhoun County Museum in Port Lavaca, Texas has a Karankawa exhibit[xvii] and a few books provide accounts of the natives.[xviii] The Boy Scouts of America operate Camp Karankawa, named after these people and is located on Lake Corpus Christi, northwest of the city.[xix]

Prior to the 1830s, written history about the region is scarce. The area surrounding Corpus Christi was sparsely populated and at times in its early history the fledgling community was almost deserted.[xx] As the few remaining native peoples of the area were previously driven south and west, the town of Corpus Christi was formed during the mid-1800s. While earlier attempts were made to establish outposts in the area, the first permanent trading post was successfully established on Corpus Christi Bay in 1839.[xxi] A trader and developer, Colonel Henry Lawrence Kinney (1814-1862), founded Nuecestown and Kinney's Rancho which would become part of the City of Corpus Christi.[xxii] In the mid-1840s a Post Office was established, and the town of Corpus Christi became the seat of the newly formed Nueces County in 1846, just one year after Texas became a U.S. state. The city was not officially incorporated until February 16, 1852 and by 1860 reached a population of 1,200.[xxiii]

Situated on the Texas Coastal Plains, Corpus Christi is at the heart of the Coastal Bend Region. The name Coastal Bend is derived from the distinctive angular shape of the Texas shoreline as it runs in a more longitudinal orientation south beginning roughly at the point of Corpus Christi Bay and the northernmost portion of Padre Island. The area has naturally sparse vegetation with mesquite trees, cactus, and a variety of grasses being the prominent flora. Barrier islands, notably Mustang Island and Padre Island, create a series of shallow wetlands and bays. Some of these wetlands now lie inside the modern-day city limits. The area is well-known for its fishing, marine life, and numerous bird species (resident and migratory).[xxiv]

Port of Corpus Christi, Texas with Freighter Passing Under Drawbridge
Lee, Russell (1939). Library of Congress, LC-USF33- 012013-MS [P&P] LOT 604

The trading posts established at the onset of the community are indicative of how the industrial base of the city would develop. Interest in the area as a port dates to 1828 when Mexican authorities considered the prospect but ultimately did not develop the area. Corpus Christi relies heavily on its port for trade and commerce such as with oil refining and the production of petroleum-based products. Oil is supplied from well fields in south and west Texas.[xxv]

Perhaps the most significant development in ocean bound trade were improvements made to the natural port to create a deep-water port for the city. The project included breakwaters provided by state funding and deepening of the ship channel as provided by federal funding. Government support was achieved through a hard-fought battle to persuade the Army Corps of Engineers to approve the port project.

The push included years of persistent lobbying by civic leaders such as manager of the King Ranch Robert J. Kleberg (1853-1932), and Henry Pomeroy "Roy" Miller (1883-1946) Mayor of Corpus Christi

(1913-1919), among others. To complete this project, local voters over-whelming approved tax bonds to provide the local funding portion as a necessary match to the federal appropriation. Port improvements were completed on September 14, 1926.[xxvi] The Port of Corpus Christi as a formal entity was formed that same year and has grown to become the third largest port in the nation based on total revenue tonnage. Civic leaders originally envisioned the Port of Corpus Christi to be largely used for agricultural products. However, oil production in the state has led the port to largely focus on input and output capacity for this in-dustry. In the late 1900s, pipeline infrastructure development brought petroleum to the city for refinement.[xxvii]

In the 1870s, railroads came to Corpus Christi as the city served as a main stop between San Antonio and the Rio Grande Valley. These rail lines were instrumental in supplying cattle from area ranches to North-ern markets. By 1914, four rail lines served the city.[xxviii]

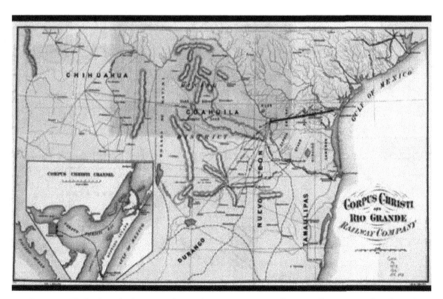

Corpus Christi and Rio Grande Railway Company, [Map of proposed railroad between Laredo and Corpus Christi and its connections with Mexico] (1873)
Bien , Julius (Contributor). Library of Congress, G4031.P3 1873.85

As home to several refineries and industries that produce oil-based products, Corpus Christi is an increasingly important logistics center for the oil industry. As U.S. petroleum production increased and due to a change in federal regulations in late 2015 to allow the export of crude oil, Corpus Christi became the largest crude oil export hub in the nation.[xxix][xxx]

Mexican American War

The proximity near the border and attachment to the Gulf of Mexico has led Corpus Christi to have a strong and enduring military presence. Several branches of the military have played a historically important role and remain an integral part of the region today. The U.S. military's ties with Corpus Christi began as soon as Texas became the 38th U.S. State. In 1845, General Zachary Taylor encamped with 3,500 troops in the area in preparation for the Mexican American War. The declaration of war would not occur until April 25, 1846 but disputes leading to the conflict were gestating much earlier and culminated as Texas gained its statehood.[xxxi][xxxii]

A major source of conflict was the boundary dispute between Mexico and the U.S. The Nueces River, which flows into Nueces Bay and the adjoining Corpus Christi Bay, was claimed by Mexico as the northern border of their territory. However, the newly annexed State of Texas and the U.S. countered that the more southerly Rio Grande River was the border between the two nations. Thus, hundreds of square miles between the two rivers, referred to as the "Trans-Nueces," was disputed territory.[xxxiii] Even though the area was sparsely populated, the Mexican government strongly contested any claim that this area belonged to Texas.[xxxiv]

The settlement of Corpus Christi, with its strong ties to the Republic of Texas, served as partial justification for the U.S. claim to the Trans Nueces. Thus, the encampment of Taylor in Corpus Christi was both symbolic and strategic. After seven months of training and preparation, Taylor marched his army south towards Mexico signaling a start to the major combat phase of the war. In addition to Taylor, who would become the 12th U.S. President, many future Confederate and Union officers would spend most of a year in Corpus Christi preparing for this action. These included Ulysses S. Grant, then a lieutenant in the U.S. Army, who would become the Union Commander during the Civil War and later the 18th U.S. President. The departure of Taylor's army left Corpus Christi almost deserted and ended the economic boon which the stationing of troops had brought to the city. However, the retirement of many U.S. veterans of the Mexican American War to Corpus Christi led to a resurgence following the war.[xxxv]

U.S. Army Encampment in Corpus Christi
Daniel P Whiting (Library of Congress)

The Mexican American War ended in a decisive victory for the U.S. with Mexico suffering a substantial loss of military and civilian lives and territory. Ultimately, the U.S. Army under General Winfield Scott occupied the capital of Mexico City. The conflict formally ended with the signing of the Treaty of Guadalupe Hidalgo on February 2, 1848 in the

Basilica of Guadalupe at Villa Hidalgo, Mexico. The treaty set the Rio Grande River, not the Nueces River, as the border between the U.S. and Mexico. Further, the treaty ceded a vast amount of Mexican territory to the U.S., resulting in the formation of California, Arizona, Nevada, Utah, and parts of several other states in exchange for a small payment. This treaty placed the Corpus Christi over 150 miles north of the Mexico-U.S. border.[xxxvi]

The Civil War

Smuggling had occurred around Corpus Christi since before the establishment of the Republic of Texas. The Confederate States of America would use the port for smuggling goods in defiance of the naval blockade imposed by U.S. (Union) forces during the American Civil War (1861-1865). Corpus Christi was bombarded in August 1862 with Confederate batteries exchanging fire with Union ships. Mustang Island was occupied by Union forces under General Nathaniel P. Banks in late 1863 during maneuvers designed to cut off the smuggling of goods. The Civil War and associated blockade would result in many people leaving Corpus Christi and mark a low point in the development of the city. The Civil War also marked the second time that the area had been shaped by military operations due to its geographic importance. The military would further shape the use of Ward Island, the mission of the university, and the larger Corpus Christi community in the middle of the 20th Century.[xxxvii][xxxviii]

Post-Civil War and the Interwar Period

Following the Civil War, military interest in the area would wane with a decades-long lull in activity. In the 75 years between the Civil War and World War II, development of Ward Island never fully materialized. Some interest in private development of the island existed, but no large scale projects ever successfully took hold.[xxxix]

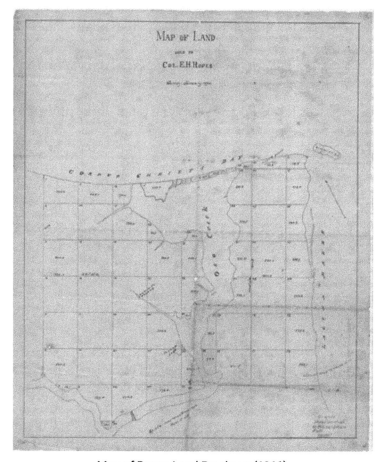

Map of Ropes Land Purchase (1911)
*Charles H. F von Blucher Family Papers, Collection 4, Mary and Jeff
Bell Library, Special Collections and Archives Department, Texas
A&M University-Corpus Christi*

In 1889, Elihu Harrison Ropes (1845-1898) of New York attempted to develop several projects in Corpus Christi including port improvements, rail line extensions, and industrial development. The basis for these developments would rest on the improvement of the natural port of Corpus Christi into a deep-water port. Thus, Ropes went about dredging a channel that would permit oceangoing vessels to sail the 32 miles from Corpus Christi Bay to Aransas Pass. His work set off a real estate frenzy known as the "Ropes Bubble." Prices skyrocketed and the resulting economic bubble ultimately led to financial ruin for Ropes, his investors, and the Corpus Christi community.[xl] This work did lay an important foundation for later port improvements in the following decades. However, Ropes was not able to leverage his efforts into the industrial development he had envisioned.

Part of Ropes' larger development plans included the property that would become Ward Island and surrounding land for a total of 1,280-acres. Ropes slated the island tract for residential real estate development.[xli] Rope's entire project was abandoned after several setbacks and the onset of the Financial Panic of 1893. This led not only to failure of the development but largely contributed to the personal financial ruin of Ropes. He returned to New York having lost his entire investment and passed away destitute in 1898.[xlii] However, while Ropes was ultimately not successful in his development, his grandiose vision for Corpus Christi, as both an industrial center served by a deep-water port and a desirable sub-topical residential locale, served as a catalyst for others to work towards similar visions.

John C. Ward purchased the island in 1892 for the purpose of a real estate development consisting of an exclusive resort community. He paid $1,448 for the island and named it Ward Island after himself. He did not develop it due to an economic downturn and only remained in the area for less than two years.[xliii][xliv] Ward moved with his family to Beaumont, Texas after abandoning the project. Even though he did not fully develop the land or remain a resident for long, the island has retained his name which has persistently stuck even as ownership has changed and official action to re-name it has occurred.[xlv]

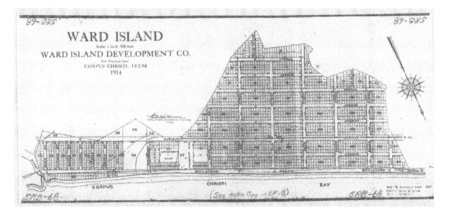

Development Plan for Ward Island (1914)
Special Collections and Archives, Mary and Jeff Bell Library, Texas A&M University-Corpus Christi

In 1914, plans for an amusement park on Ward Island were made. There was to be an electric trolley line running eight miles from the town center to the Island. However, in 1916 a hurricane disrupted work and again the island was not developed.[xlvi]

After the failure of any large-scale development to take hold, Ward Island remained a destination for hunting and fishing for several decades.[xlvii] There is documentation that some families resided on the island and small-scale, tourism-related businesses were established.[xlviii] Cotton was farmed on about half of the island beginning in the 1920s. The first documented use of the island for aviation purposes was in 1924. The Elks-Kindred Flying Circus visited Corpus Christi and performed on Ward Island for thousands of spectators.[xlix] The following year, the Garver Flying Circus also performed on the island.[l] The flying circus featured not only the new technology of the day, the airplane, but acrobatics and stunts by performers. The selection of Ward Island for the circus emphasizes the lack of large-scale development of the property and also suggests that the island was accessible and notable in that thousands made their way to attend these performances.

A few small businesses, fishing piers, and a goat herd were present on the island leading into the 1940s when the military would take over the property.[li] The goat herd had been problematic for landing and taking off for the airplanes during the 1924 air circus performance.[lii] The goats would--sadly--be removed by the U.S. Army.

World War II

As World War II raged, the Roosevelt administration took action to increase the training facilities for U.S. Army pilots. To further this mission, a $25 million appropriation funded the Naval Air Station at Corpus Christi in 1940, and the base was commissioned in July 1942. Six stations related to the mission of naval training were located in South Texas including sites at Kingsville, Beeville, Flour Bluff, and south of Corpus Christi. These installations trained not only aviators but other key positions that would prove instrumental for building the U.S. Army Air Corps and ultimately winning the war. Advanced training was provided to service members of the Navy, Marines, Coast Guard, and the Royal Canadian Air Force.[liii]

Aviation Cadet at the Naval Air Base, Corpus Christi, Texas
Harlem, Howard R. Library of Congress, LC-USW36- 7056

The naval bases included Ward Island which would house a training facility called the Naval Air Technical Training Center Ward Island or the Radio Material School.[liv][lv] In 1942, the government took over the property and paid $143,406 for 23 parcels of land, thus consolidating all of Ward Island under government ownership for military use.[lvi]

Mrs. Irma Lee McElroy Paints the American Insignia on Airplane Wings at the Naval Air Base, Corpus Christi, Texas (1942)
Library of Congress. LC-USW36-387

The school that was built on the island was a top-secret training facility for the newly implemented radar technology. While the installation was not to be discussed during the first years of its existence, a large military presence was established. Access to the base was strictly controlled, and the property was encircled by a security fence. Use of the word 'radar' by cadets who were training on Ward Island was an offense punishable by court-martial. Even the Marines guarding the facility did not know what was taking place inside. This level of secrecy highlights the importance of radar to the Allies during the war. The Ward Island facility was critical in this effort through training radar technicians.[lvii]

At the conclusion of the war, the base had 67 buildings including gymnasiums, dormitories, classrooms, swimming pools, storage facilities, and an administration building. Ultimately, 10,000 technicians would graduate from the Aviation Electronics Training School.[lviii][lix]

The winding down of military operations following World War II diminished the need for training facilities. The military no longer required the physical space that it had during the war and ultimately Ward Island was surplused for the purpose of a university. The radio station and the 2,300 students still based at Ward Island were moved to Millington, Tennessee, near Memphis, in September 1947.[lx][lxi]

"Sailor and Girl" (Corpus Christi, 1943)
Vachon, John. Library of Congress LC-USW3-033949-D [P&P]

NAS-Corpus Christi

While Ward Island was to change from naval control to serve as a university, the adjacent Naval Air Station Corpus Christi (NAS Corpus Christi) remained a military installation. This base is to the east of Ward Island in the Flour Bluff area of Corpus Christi. Access via Ocean Drive between Ward Island and the naval installation is restricted and a security gate prohibits unauthorized traffic onto the base. Some operations of the base have changed over time, yet the core mission of training pilots has been consistent since its founding in 1941.[lxii] U.S. Army maintenance operations began on the base in 1961 as the Navy had shut down a major repair facility on the station two years earlier.[lxiii]

Enlisted Service Members Arrive in Corpus Christi, Bay (1972)
Dr Hector P Garcia Papers, Collection 5, Box 432, Folder 5. Special Collections and Archives, Mary and Jeff Bell Library, Texas A&M University-Corpus Christi

In 2021, a robust military presence is stationed at NAS Corpus Christi. In addition to U.S. Navy aviator training, the Army, Marine Corps, Customs and Border Protection Service, and Coast Guard all have operations on the base. The army maintains much of its fleet of rotary wing aircraft at the facility while Customs and Border Patrol uses the base to operate Unmanned Aerial Systems for surveillance.[lxiv] The retired aircraft carrier *USS Lexington* (CVT-16), berthed in Corpus Christi Bay as a floating museum, is a fitting tribute to the era that led to the modern development of the military in the city.[lxv]

Ward Island, with its facilities built for the purpose of instruction and quarters, made a logical site for an institution of higher education. However, Ward Island was not the only facility among the South Texas naval bases to be de-commissioned. Three retired naval sites in South Texas would play a role in the development of the Island University.

The Island

Ward Island has been home to a university since 1947, beginning with the University of Corpus Christi (UCC). Through several name changes, the university has provided educational opportunities for tens of thousands of students. Perhaps the most unique feature about the university is its geography. Those with close ties to the university may tend to forget that the tranquil, calming, and peaceful surroundings inherent with the coastal setting are a pleasure that falls well outside of the norm. Not everyone gets to travel to an island to work as a faculty or staff member or attend classes as a student. Indeed, the university is the only one in the nation to occupy its own island.

Many universities are defining physical landmarks of their communities, as is the case for the largest Texas A&M University system institution in College Station. The Bryan/College Station area has built up around the university. Other system schools have developed and grown as integral parts of smaller cities as with Tarleton State University and Texas A&M University-Commerce. A more recent trend focuses on bringing educational opportunity to downtown in the cases of The University of North Texas-Dallas and the downtown campus of The University of Texas at San Antonio. In contrast, a feeling of detachment from the community can occur on the campuses of Texas A&M University-San Antonio or Texas A&M International University in Laredo. These campuses were more recently built on large tracts of land to accommodate for growth. The Island University has physical restrictions imposed by the surrounding bays and estuaries as well as height restrictions due to flight training conducted at the nearby naval air station.

As with the Island University, campuses that are not immediately adjacent to their host communities may experience a sense of detachment from important stakeholders. The geography has made it at least more physically challenging to integrate into the larger Corpus Christi community. The campus has little commercial activity surrounding it to serve students, faculty, and staff. There are few stores, bars, or restaurants near the university that might serve as student "hangouts." There is not the option to easily "go grab lunch" off campus in between classes by taking a short walk across the street. For instance, students attending The University of Texas at Austin often walk across Guadalupe Street to visit any number of restaurants and stores just across from the campus. As most students do not live on the island, they must journey to and from campus on Ocean Drive, the single route on and off the campus as road access to the adjacent military base is restricted. Even while there may be a physical distance, there is a strong community attachment. Without nearby commercial centers, students from the university tend to disperse into the community to work, volunteer, worship, shop, and reside. Islanders have become an integral part of the Corpus Christi community. Many students are from the area while many others choose to remain in the region after graduation.

The support of Corpus Christi and surrounding communities has been vital to the founding and development of TAMU-CC. The community was instrumental in attracting an upstart private Baptist college to Corpus Christi. Through several name changes and shifts in the mission of the institution, this support has remained steadfast and in certain cases critical for the very continuation of the institution.

Corpus Christi Bay at Ward Island (n.d.)
Texas A&M University-Corpus Christi

References

[i] About Us. (2021). Texas A&M University-Corpus Christi https://www.tamucc.edu/about/

[ii] Howard, R. (1947, March 30). New Beeville College Dean experienced school builder. Corpus Christi Caller, p. 17.

[iii] Wrotenbery, C. R. (1998). Baptist Island College. Fort Worth, Texas: Eakin Press.

[iv] Wrotenbery, C. R. (1998). Baptist Island College. Fort Worth, Texas: Eakin

[v] Naval Air Station Corpus Christi. (2020, August 22). Commander, Navy Installations Command https://www.cnic.navy.mil/regions/cnrse/installations/nas_corpus_christi.html

[vi] O'Rear, M. J. (2009). Storm over the Bay: The people of Corpus Christi and their port. College Station: Texas A&M University

[vii] Long, (n.d.). Corpus Christi, TX. Handbook of Texas Online. Texas State Historical Association. https://tshaonline.org/hand book/online/articles/hdc03

[viii] Lipscomb, C. A. (n.d.). Karankawa Indians. Handbook of Texas Online. Texas State Historical Association. https://tshaon org/handbook/online/articles/bmk0 5

[ix] Karankawa Indians. (2020, August 29). Calhoun County Museum. https://calhouncountymuseum.org/exhibits/karankawa-indians/

[x] Lipscomb, A. (n.d.). Karankawa Indians. Handbook of Texas Online. Texas State Historical Association. https:/ /tshaonline.org/handbook/online/articles/bmk0 5

[xi] Givens, M., & Moloney, J. (2011). Corpus Christi: A history. Corpus Christi, TX: Nueces Press.

[xii] Wolff, (1969). The Karankawa Indians: Their conflict with the White man in Texas. *Ethnohistory.* Duke University Press.

[xiii] Karankawa Indians. (2020, August 29). Calhoun County Mu-
https://calhouncountymuseum.org/exhibits/karankawa-indi-ans/

[xiv] Givens, M., & Moloney, J. (2011). Corpus Christi: A history.
Corpus Christi, TX: Nueces Press.

[xv] Wolff, (1969). The Karankawa Indians: Their conflict with the
White man in Texas. *Ethnohistory*. Duke University Press.

[xvi] Lipscomb, C. A. (n.d.). Karankawa Indians. Handbook of
Texas Online. Texas State Historical Association. https://tshaon org/
handbook/online/articles/bmk0S

[xvii] Karankawa (2020, August 29). Calhoun County Museum.
https://calhouncountymuseum.org/exhibits/karankawa-indians/

[xviii] Gatschet, Albert S. The Karankawa Indians, The Coast People of Texas., book, 1891; Cambridge, Massachusetts. (https://texashis-
tory.unt.edu/ark:/67531/metapth29754/: accessed October 14, 2021),
University of North Texas Libraries, The Portal to Texas History,
https://texashistory.unt.edu; crediting Star of the Republic Museum.

[xix] Camp Karankawa. (2020, August 29). Boy Scouts of America
Bay Area http://www.bacbsa.org/camp-karankawa/69179

[xx] Givens, M., & Moloney, J. (2011). Corpus Christi: A history.
Corpus Christi, TX: Nueces Press.

[xxi] Long, C. (n.d.). Corpus Christi, TX. Handbook of Texas
Online. Texas State Historical Association. https://tshaonline.org/
handbook/online/articles/hdc03

[xxii] Givens, M., & Moloney, J. (2011). Corpus Christi: A history.
Corpus Christi, TX: Nueces Press.

[xxiii] Long, C. (n.d.). Corpus Christi, TX. Handbook of Texas
Online. Texas State Historical Association. https://tshaonline.org/
handbook/ online/articles/hdc03

[xxiv] Hickman, G. C. (1995). A field guide to Ward Island, Corpus
Christi, College Station, Texas: Texas A&M University.

[xxv] Givens, M., & Moloney, J. (2011). Corpus Christi: A history.
Corpus Christi, TX: Nueces Press.

[xxvi] O'Rear, M. (2009). Storm over the Bay: The people of Corpus Christi and their port. College Station: Texas A&M University Press.

[xxvii] The Energy Port of the Americas. (2020, September 5). Port of Corpus Christi. https:/ /portofcc.com/we-are-the energy-port-of-the-americas/

[xxviii] Long, C. (n.d.). Corpus Christi, Handbook of Texas Online. Texas State Historical Association. https://tshaonline.org/ handbook/online/articles/hdc03

[xxix] Chapa, S. (2019, June 11). Report: Port of Corpus Christi to become top S. crude oil export hub. Houston Chronicle: https://www.chron.com/business/energy/article/Report-Port-of-Corpus-Christi-to-become-top-U-S-13968069.php

[xxx] Long, (n.d.). Corpus Christi, TX. Handbook of Texas Online. Texas State Historical Association. https://tshaonline.org/hand book/online/articles/hdc03

[xxxi] Long, C. (n.d.). Corpus Christi, TX. Handbook of Texas Online. Texas State Historical Association. https://tshaonline.org/ handbook/online/articles/hdc03

[xxxii] Givens, M., & Moloney, J. (2011). Corpus Christi: A history. Corpus Christi, TX: Nueces Press.

[xxxiii] Library of The Changing Mexican-U.S. Border. https://blogs.loc.gov/maps/2015/12/the-changing-mexico-u-s-bor der/

[xxxiv] Givens, M., & Moloney, J. (2011). Corpus Christi: A history. Corpus Christi, TX: Nueces Press.

[xxxv] Givens, M., & Moloney, J. (2011). Corpus Christi: A history. Corpus Christi, TX: Nueces Press.

[xxxvi] Library of Congress. The Changing Mexican-U.S. https://blogs.loc.gov/maps/2015 /12/ the-changing-mexico-u-s-bor der/

[xxxvii] Leatherwood, A. (2010, June 15). Naval Air Station, Corpus Christi. Handbook of Texas Online. Texas State Historical

Association https://tshaonline.org/handbook/online/articles/qbn01

[xxxviii] Givens, M., & Moloney, J. (2011). Corpus Christi: A history. Corpus Christi, TX: Nueces Press.

[xxxix] Hickman, C. (1995). A field guide to Ward Island, Corpus Christi, Texas. College Station, Texas: Texas A&M University.

[xl] Givens, M. (2013, February 6). What was the big secret on John Ward's island? Corpus Christi Caller-Times.

[xli] Nueces County (2020). Elihu Harrison Ropes. Nueces County Historical Commission. https://www.nuecesco.com/county services/county-boards/historical-commission/elihu-harrison-ropes

[xlii] Nueces County (2020). Elihu Harrison Ropes. Nueces County Historical Commission. https://www.nuecesco.com/county services/county-boards/historical-commission/elihu-harrison-ropes

[xliii] Ward Island is no more; name changed. (1953, May 28). Corpus Christi Caller, p. 47.

[xliv] Givens, M. (2013, February 6). What was the big secret on John Ward's island? Corpus Christi Caller-Times.

[xlv] Givens, M. (2013, February 6). What was the big secret on John Ward's island? Corpus Christi Caller-Times.

[xlvi] Givens, M. (2013, February 6). What was the big secret on John Ward's island? Corpus Christi Caller-Times.

[xlvii] Hickman, G. C. (1995). A field guide to Ward Island, Corpus Christi, Texas. College Station, Texas: Texas A&M University.

[xlviii] Warranty deeds filed for record. (1930, October 17). Corpus Christi Caller and Daily Herald, p. 12.

[xlix] Elks-Kindred Flying Circus at Ward Island. (1924, October 27). Corpus Christi Caller and Daily Herald, p. 1.

[l] Garver Flying Circus. (1925, March 29). Corpus Christi Caller and Daily Herald. Corpus Christi, Texas.

[li] Hickman, G. C. (1995). A field guide to Ward Island, Corpus Christi, Texas. College Station, Texas: Texas A&M University.

[lii] Elks-Kindred Flying Circus at Ward Island. (1924, October 27). Corpus Christi Caller and Daily Herald, p. 1.

[liii] Delaney, N. C. (2013, May). Corpus Christi's 'University of the Air'. U.S. Naval Institute. https:/ /www.usni.org/magazines/naval history-magazine/2013/may/corpus-christis-university-air

[liv] Hickman, G. C. (1995). A field guide to Ward Island, Corpus Christi, Texas. College Station, Texas: Texas A&M University.

[lv] Leatherwood, A. (2010, June 15). Naval Air Station, Corpus Christi. Handbook of Texas Online. Texas State Historical Association. https:// tshaonline.org/handbook/online/articles/qbn01

[lvi] Givens, M. (2013, February 6). What was the big secret on John Ward's island? Corpus Christi Caller-Times.

[lvii] Delaney, N. C. (2013, May). Corpus Christi's 'University of the Air'. U.S. Naval Institute. https:/ /www.usni.org/magazines/naval history-magazine/2013/may/corpus-christis-university-air

[lviii] Hickman, G. C. (1995). A field guide to Ward Island, Corpus Christi, Texas. College Station, Texas: Texas A&M University.

[lix] Rosser,]. (1978, October 12). CCSU worker must move after years on campus. Corpus Christi Caller, p. 66.

[lx] Branning, C. (1989, January 12). Baptist opened university. Corpus Christi Caller-Times, p. 67.

[lxi] Wrotenbery, C. R. (1998). Baptist Island College. Fort Worth, Texas: Eakin Press.

[lxii] Naval Air Station Corpus Christi. (2020, August 22). Commander, Navy Installations Command Notification. https://www.cnic.navy.mil/regions/cnrse/installations/nas_corpus_christi.html

[lxiii] Leatherwood, A. (2010,June 15). Naval Air Station, Corpus Christi. Handbook of Texas Online. Texas State Historical Association. https:// tshaonline.org/handbook/online/articles/qbn01

[lxiv]Naval Air Station Corpus Christi. (2020, August 22). Commander, Navy Installations Command Notification. https://www.cnic.navy.mil/regions/cnrse/installations/nas_corpus_christi.html

[lxv] Delaney, N. C. (2013, May). Corpus Christi's 'University of the Air'. U.S. Naval Institute. https:/ /www.usni.org/magazines/naval history-magazine/2013/may/corpus-christis-university-air

Building a University

Aerial View of Ward Island (1948)
*Mary and Jeff Bell Library, Special Collections and Archives Department, Texas A&M
University-Corpus Christi*

Plans for what would decades later become Texas A&M University Corpus Christi (TAMU-CC) began in earnest in the mid-1940s. The original plans hardly resemble the university as it stands today. The name, location, and key stakeholders associated with TAMU-CC were different. The type of students to be served, as envisioned by early university founders, might now be considered only a slice of the large and diverse student body that now calls TAMU-CC home. Over decades, the Island University has been re-shaped, often due to pressures well beyond its control. However, the fundamental mission to provide South Texas with access to an educational institution remains true from the earliest discussions about starting a college through today.

U.S. Emergence

World War II defined a generation and transformed the U.S. into a global superpower. Through the period leading up to the war, the U.S. had a small military. There was little necessity for a standing army on the European model. The need to defend the U.S. border was minimal as its neighbors were allies and also had small militaries. The U.S. was only a minor player in terms of imperial expansion unlike Great Britain, France, Italy, Spain, and other European nations with their numerous overseas territories. For instance, at its zenith, the British Empire controlled a vast territory on which the "sun never set" as it covered a quarter of the World's landmass. However, the U.S. was a sleeping giant in terms of industrial capacity. The nation's large population would prove critical for building the armies necessary to fight a global conflict. Following World War II, a reordering of world powers would catapult the U.S. to the forefront of global affairs and commerce.

The war brought about significant social changes in the U.S. After the war, conditions were right for a historic expansion of higher education. Many of the common occurrences of life had been placed on hold as the U.S. engaged in the singular national mission of winning the war. Millions of young Americans had been called into uniformed service while millions more toiled to build the instruments of war not only for U.S. soldiers, sailors, and marines but also for U.S. allies. Great

Britain relied heavily on U.S. goods to continue the fight in Europe against Germany and its ally, Italy. The U.S. had been supplying food and war material to Great Britain under the lend/lease agreement even before the U.S. was attacked at Pearl Harbor and entered the war in late 1941. A monumental effort to build everything from Liberty Ships for transporting goods to ammunition, tanks, jeeps, and aircraft shifted U.S. industrial capacity towards filling these enormous demands. U.S. consumers found limited availability of products ranging from butter to automobiles, as goods were either diverted for war time use or factories converted from making consumer products to war material.

After the war, returning soldiers were eager to gain an education to build their careers and provide for their families. The idealistic middle class family--which lived in the suburbs, had an American-made car in the drive, and enjoyed many modern conveniences--began to take shape. In order to live this dream, the post-war generation needed jobs built on knowledge learned through higher education.

Millions of post-war marriages and a subsequent increase in births led to the term "baby boomers." This term would describe a generation of post-war American children who were born into a much different world than before the war. Women, with a newfound independence in part due to wide-spread wartime employment outside the home, were beginning to enroll in college in record numbers.

As U.S. firms reverted production to consumer goods, they found global demand to be very high. During the war years, people had not been able to buy appliances, cars, or obtain a new set of tires. Once the war ended, groceries and fuel for cars were no longer rationed. Americans were able to spend freely, and they did. The pent-up demand, coupled with disposable income available to the bourgeoning middle class, led to strong sales of a wide range of products. Sales included many items that were new additions to most households such as small appliances and importantly the television, which represented an entirely new medium of communication. Americans took their cars to drive-ins and on road trips for vacation.

The U.S. had learned from mistakes made following the Great War (World War I) when soldiers were released back into the workforce with little provision to assist with this often-difficult transition. The abrupt dismissal of troops and lack of assistance for finding jobs or to pursue training had proved to be a major public policy blunder. After World War II, national leaders were determined to provide for a better transition back to civilian life for veterans. Service members were released more gradually from military ranks and benefits to assist with transition were provided. One way this was accomplished was by providing major financial support to help millions of service members attend college through the Servicemen's Readjustment Act of 1944 (G.I. Bill). This program was constituted to pay the cost of earning a degree for those who had served at least 90 days in uniform.[i] These factors attributed to a high demand for college level educational programs. Thus, during this period many governmental and nonprofit entities were engaged in helping to fill this need through the founding and expansion of trade schools, colleges, and universities across the U.S.

Founding a University

The Baptist General Convention of Texas (BGCT) had been significantly involved in the higher education landscape in Texas prior to World War II. A forerunner of the BGCT, the Union Baptist Association, had established Baylor University in 1845 with approval from the Congress of the Republic of Texas. Baylor was originally located in Independence, Texas moving to Waco in 1885 in part due to the city's access to a railroad line. Baylor would become the largest and most notable BGCT-affiliated university in Texas.[ii]

The BGCT also established Hardin-Simmons University in Abilene, Howard Payne University in Brownwood, Wayland Baptist University in Plainview, East Texas Baptist University in Marshall, and the University of Mary Hardin-Baylor in Belton. Each of these universities were founded decades before World War II. With the increased demand for higher education, BGCT members saw an opportunity to expand the footprint of faith-based education across Texas. None of the existing

Baptist institutions were in South Texas. Beyond filing this regional void, many BGCT members felt that a presence in South Texas could draw students from Houston and San Antonio. The BGCT saw multiple benefits to this type of expansion including to their ministry. Baptist educational institutions not only provided higher education, but they also served to educate future ministers, and the institutions themselves served as a ministry for young people during the formative years of their lives. These institutions were viewed not only as universities but as missions that promoted religious instruction and the Baptist faith.[iii]

Beyond funding provided to veterans to gain education through the G.I. Bill, the government took steps to ensure that an adequate number of institutions existed to provide education. An incentive for creating a new university was to repurpose former military bases for educational use. Hundreds of military bases around the nation had been quickly built as part of the massive war effort. The bases were attractive to the BGCT and other entities as the government was trying to relinquish the properties and therefore offered financially attractive lease terms. The military did impose strict terms over the use of the buildings and land, as they wanted to preserve the right to reclaim the property and facilities should a need arise. South Texas had several surplused facilities as it had been an aviation training center with several fields and bases scattered around the region. Many of these were made available to local governments and other entities soon after the war.

One proposal was to repurpose Chase Field just east of Beeville, Texas as the site for a new Baptist University. Early advocates for this plan were primarily clergy from the Beeville area and Houston, 200 miles to the northeast. The strongest advocate for these plans was Rev. Aubria Allen Sanders, Sr., the pastor of the First Baptist Church of Beeville. Sanders recognized that a BGCT-affiliated college in Beeville could advance the mission to bring a Baptist institution of higher education to South Texas. He further recognized that the closing of the Naval Air Station at Chase Field would be a sizable economic loss for the Beeville community that might be partly offset by the founding of a university.[iv][v]

Beeville was a small city northwest of Corpus Christi and southeast of San Antonio. Sanders strongly advocated for Chase Field to be the home of the newly proposed college. Events moved quickly as during the spring of 1947 Sanders took a leave of absence as pastor to devote himself full-time to founding the college. Sanders was not only the visionary be hind the school but also its first capital campaign chairperson and college board secretary.[vi][vii]

Rev. Aubria Sanders
1949 Silver King Mary and Jeff Bell Library,
Special Collections and Archives
Department, Texas A&M University-Corpus
Christi.

Wallace Bassett, the BGCT Board President, tasked Rev. Dr. S. Hutcherson and Rev. Dr. E. Hermond Westmoreland with determining the feasibility of a new Baptist university in South Texas. Both men were pastors of churches in Houston, Texas. Westmoreland was the pastor of South Main Street Baptist Church while Hutcherson was pastor of Trinity Baptist Church. There was not consensus between the two on where to locate the college as a major concern was that the Chase Field site was too large for a start-up college. However, the BGCT would ultimately approve the Chase Field location and further determined that the university should be a new school, not a branch of one of the existing Baptist colleges as had been discussed.[viii]

The ATC Board of Directors was filled mostly by ministers with few having extensive experience in higher education. Hutcherson was selected as the first president of the university and resigned his post as pastor at Trinity Baptist Church. Raymond M. Cavness was selected as the first academic Dean of the College. He was in the minority among early college leaders for having worked directly in higher education as both a faculty member and administrator. However, Cavness was given a leave of absence in June 1947, mere months into the job, as the demands of his position would not allow him to work to complete his graduate degree. Chairman of the Religious Studies Department John Cobb would become acting

University of Corpus Christi President Rev. E.S. Hutcherson
1949 Silver King. Mary and Jeff Bell Library, Special Collections and Archives Department, Texas A&M University-Corpus Christi

dean. Cavness would ultimately resign in September 1948. Hutcherson would only serve as president through the first academic year, leaving the post in 1948.[ix]

Arts and Technology College

Arts and Technology College (ATC) was formed with a decidedly Baptist underpinning. Contrary to what the name might have suggested, degrees focused on the ministry would be an important offering of the new college. Attendance at weekly chapel, as well as student behavioral expectations helped to define the college experience for students at all BGCT universities including ATC.[x]

Students Attending Chapel (Circa 1950s)
Special Collections and Archives, Mary and Jeff Bell Library, Texas A&M University-Corpus Christi

Chase Field was one of six naval airfield installations built in South Texas at the start of World War II.[xi] The location was challenging as the base was somewhat physically disconnected from the city. Students and faculty who lived on campus would have to make the short drive into Beeville for any services that did not exist on site. Chase Field did have many of the necessary buildings and facilities for a college to start operations in a short amount of time. Among the 104 buildings were dormitories, dining halls, recreational facilities, and an administration building.[xii]

The ATC name was never intended to be permanent. It was adopted somewhat hastily with the intention of determining a more appropriate name later. Indeed, the name itself invokes a bit of an identity crisis. The other universities supported by the BGCT were decidedly liberal arts colleges with large numbers of ministerial students. The "technology" portion of the ATC name was ill-defined in terms of the mission and was more a reflection of the desire to utilize the available facilities at Chase Field than a goal of the BGCT. The naval air station at Chase Field had the necessary land and facilities to offer several technology focused degrees. For instance, the 2,600 plus acre site[xiii] would have ample space to develop a farm to provide agriculture students with on-site training. However, most backers from BGCT were more concerned about advancing its core mission as a Baptist ministry than offering industry centered degrees.[xiv]

The technology and career-based programs were outside of the typical scope of a Baptist-supported school as religion and bible classes were popular. Early course offerings at ATC were to include art, bacteriology, Bible, biology, liberal arts, journalism, Greek, and zoology among others. Over time, the focus of the curriculum would shift to more career-oriented coursework and degrees such as teacher education and business became increasingly popular majors.[xv] The divide between the BGCT mission and student demand for career-focused degrees would prove an ongoing source of internal conflict.

The early obstacles faced by ATC were formidable. The schedule for founding the institution and starting classes was remarkably quick. Perhaps more troubling was that the City of Beeville was not as supportive of the project to the extent that many in the BGCT had hoped.[xvi] The BGCT expected financial support from the community, local churches, and businesses at a level that never materialized. A clause in the contract between the City of Beeville and ATC, which allowed the city to cancel the lease with 90-days notice, provided little stability and the potential for a major loss of the BGCT's investment. This clause was viewed by the BGCT as particularly unreasonable since semesters would run for longer than a three-month time frame.[xvii]

A sentiment grew that the city was just looking for another entity to assume the massive undertaking of maintaining the scores of structures and enormous track that had been Chase Field. These maintenance costs would place a heavy burden on ATC as the acreage and number of buildings far exceeded their short-term needs. The naval buildings had largely been constructed out of wood and for use as temporary structures to last the duration of the war. Thus, even buildings that were less than ten years old needed painting and significant repairs.[xviii][xix]

A difficult arrangement existed between the U.S. Navy (the owner of the property), the City of Beeville (the lease holder), and the board of directors of ATC (the tenant). Under the governance structure, the BGCT was involved as the sponsor and major financial backer of ATC. This unwieldy organizational structure was necessary to follow federal law that prohibited a religious entity from being granted surplused government property. Instead, a local government entity would act as an intermediary while the college, as a tenant, was to carry out the educational mission as desired by the U.S. Government for its decommissioned bases. Further, clauses in the contract allowed for reactivation of the properties for military use in the event of war or other need. Thus, not only could the City of Beeville exercise control over the property, so could the U.S. Government.[xx]

A major turning point for the future of the new university was rooted in tragedy when Rev. Sanders was killed in a car accident in May of 1947 mere months before the opening of ATC was set to occur in September. The accident occurred when Sanders was returning to Beeville from Houston on a fundraising trip for ATC. The untimely loss of Sanders, who was 44, was not only a difficult loss for the community, but it marked a turning point in deliberations over the location for ATC. Even as plans were made to memorialize Sanders by naming the library at Chase Field after him, the ATC location became increasingly problematic.[xxi]

Knowledge that the ATC board was disenchanted with the situation at Chase Field and looking for other potential sites to locate the school became commonly known in the summer of 1947. Further, articles suggest that within the Beeville business community there was little desire for ATC to locate at Chase Field.[xxii] In response, leaders from other communities in Central and South Texas began working to attract ATC to their own cities. Corpus Christi offered the ATC board an attractive proposal that included potential sites for locating at one of two former naval bases. The proposal pledged private and city funding to assist with the major financial outlay necessary to found a new university. The Corpus Christi offer was the most generous and the decision was made on July 25, 1947 by the ATC board to relocate there. The BGCT executive committee ratified the action in early August and students, who were slated to begin classes the following month, were notified of the change of location in a letter dated August 9th.[xxiii]

For a brief time, the university was referred to as ATC-CC (Corpus Christi), but the move quickly led to a name change from ATC to the University of Corpus Christi (UCC) for the opening of classes in fall 1947. The name was reflective not only of the new location but the standing as a four-year university with a mission to provide for a broad range of degree options beyond those of a more limited liberal arts college.[xxiv]

University of Corpus Christi Cheer Leaders with Anchor (n.d.)
Texas A&M University-Corpus Christi

The University of Corpus Christi

The Corpus Christi community was supportive of bringing a university to the city from the beginning of the process. In relation to Beeville, Corpus Christi had a much larger population of 57,301 in the city limits and 115,000 in the area at the time. The region had a large industrial base and growing business community.[xxv] As a center of commerce, Corpus Christi was better positioned to raise the necessary capital and support needed for founding a private institution. Supporters such as Guy Warren and Howard E. Butt, Sr. were early advocates for building the campus in Corpus Christi. The two families are notable as long-time advocates and supporters of UCC.[xxvi]

UCC 1949 Best All Around Girl, Hugh Delle Manahan and Best All Around Boy, Sonny Norrell

1949 Silver King. Special Collections and Archives, Mary and Jeff Bell Library, Texas A&M University-Corpus Christi

Howard E. Butt, Sr. (1895-1991) was the CEO of H-E B Grocery Store. He generously supported UCC with both his business knowledge and financial backing. Butt would serve as Chairman of the UCC Board from 1950-1966. Several important financial gifts came from the H. E. Butt Foundation for which he was the founder. His son, Howard E. Butt, Jr. (1927-2016), would also be instrumental in the development of the school. He was a strong advocate of the promotion of Christian education in Corpus Christi.[xxvii] The Warrens were local oil operators. Guy Warren would serve as president of the Corpus Christi Citizens Council which pledged to raise $250,000 to establish a permanent location for UCC.[xxviii] Warren also served on the UCC board during its final years from 1972-1974.[xxix]

While the education of ministers remained an important function of UCC, the civic leaders who were investing in the school knew the community needed programs in business and teacher preparation in addition to a liberal arts curriculum. These more career-oriented programs would prove popular with students. Further, these demands would lead to low enrollments of ministerial students as a percentage of the overall student body. The percentage of ministerial students was a key bench mark that the BGCT set for each of its sponsored universities. The rather conflicting understanding of the mission would at times create friction among the various UCC stakeholders.

University of Corpus Christi Students (Circa 1950)
Special Collections and Archives, Mary and Jeff Bell Library, Texas A&M University-Corpus Christi

In late summer of 1947, the campus was hastily moved from Chase Field to Cuddihy Field in Corpus Christi. Classes were never held at Chase Field even as investments had been made to ready the campus for students and faculty. The BGCT absorbed the losses associated with the renovations done at the base.[xxx] Just a few years later, Chase Field would be reactivated by the Navy during the Korean conflict to train jet fighter pilots. After permanent deactivation in 1993, the former Naval Air Station Chase Field property would be used for several purposes as part of the Chase Field Industrial Complex.[xxxi] Within this complex, the Texas Department of Criminal Justice occupies 304 acres for two correctional transfer facilities-West Garza and East Garza as well as the Department's regional office.[xxxii] An industrial park and a small residential development also occupy portions of the former air field. In an interesting development, the Lone Star UAS Center of Excellence & Innovation (LSUASC) of Texas A&M University-Corpus Christi operates at the site. The 8,000-foot runway, warehouses, and open area are used for testing and evaluation of Unmanned Aircraft Systems (UAS).[xxxiii]

Cuddihy Field

Newly hired faculty, administrators, and students were provided with just over a month's notice to report to Cuddihy Field, located just west of Corpus Christi, for the beginning of classes. Cuddihy Field was built in 1941 and named for U.S. Naval Aviator Lt. George Thomas Cuddihy who died in a crash of a British Bristol Bulldog test plane on November 26, 1929. Cuddihy was a 1917 graduate of the U.S. Naval Academy and one of the top naval pilots after World War I. He assisted with the formation of the navy's first fighting plane squadron. He set a seaplane world speed record in 1924 and record for flight speed in pursuit of ships in 1926. In 1927, he flew across the Andes Mountains in South America, a route Lt. James Doolittle had also flown the previous year. Also in 1927, he won the "pursuit ship race" flying at over 180 miles per hour. Cuddihy is buried in Arlington National Cemetery and was posthumously awarded the Distinguished Flying Cross.[xxxiv]

In the original pre-war plans, Cuddihy Field, Rodd Field, Cabaniss Field, and 29 other landing sites in the area would serve as auxiliary airfields for Corpus Christi Naval Air Station (NAS). As World War II called for additional aviators, fields at Kingsville and Waldron were added in 1942. Chase Field would be the last addition to the U.S. Navy's extensive training facilities in South Texas with construction beginning in early 1943.

These would be active training bases with thousands of airmen, sailors, and support staff mostly engaged in naval training activities. Over the course of World War II, over 30,000 pilots would receive flight training from NAS-Corpus Christi. At the conclusion of World War II, 2,000 service members would be stationed at Cuddihy Field, with a total of over 20,000 across all the Corpus Christi area naval facilities. In September 1945, the decision was made to continue naval operations at Cuddihy and Chase Fields in addition to the main naval air station through 1946.[xxxv]

Much of the reported news about these facilities was not over the core, and secretive, activities of the bases but rather the social life that resulted from having a large military presence in and around Corpus Christi. Boxing matches and bowling tournaments were organized among service members representing the region's naval installations. Several marriage and birth announcements noted the location of residence as "Cuddihy Field." Sports teams, such as baseball and basketball, from these stations would routinely play one another. Ward Island, the home of the radio training facility would also field a team in many of these leagues. By the end of the war, these sports leagues were well established with team names such as the Cuddihy Clippers and Ward Island TechTras. These teams would continue through 1947.[xxxvi]

Cuddihy Field (1947)
1948 Silver King. Special Collections and Archives, Mary and Jeff Bell Library, Texas A&M University-Corpus Christi

Cuddihy Field was an 803-acre site used for basic and advanced flight training with four 5,000-foot runways, large hangars, and auxiliary buildings. The former airfield lies a few miles south of the present day Corpus Christi International Airport and 13-miles from downtown Corpus Christi by automobile.

Preparations for the former military station took place in the month leading to the official start of classes on September 15, 1947. Enrollment for the the first semester at UCC was 312 students, including 63 prospective preachers and 97 veterans, taught by 26 faculty.[xxxvii]

UCC Students Exercise on the Cuddihy Field Campus (1947)
1948 Silver King. Special Collections and Archives, Mary and Jeff Bell Library, Texas A&M University-Corpus Christi

Faculty had already been hired for programs designed to be offered at the Chase Field campus. Some of these programs were perhaps better suited for Chase Field but were still offered after the move to Cuddihy Field. Perhaps the most puzzling was the agriculture program as there would no longer be space for a university farm at either of the two prospective Corpus Christi locations. The move also placed the school within 40 miles of Texas College of Arts & Industries in Kingsville (later Texas A&M University-Kingsville) which was better positioned to offer agriculture programs given its relationship with and proximity to the expansive King Ranch.[xxxviii] In 1954, UCC would receive a gift of 100 acres near Robstown from Mr. and Mrs. M. G. Perry for the purpose of agricultural training.[xxxix] The agricultural program was designed to improve agricultural practice as opposed to training teachers. In this way, the program deviated from many of the other more liberal arts, business, or education focused programs. University leaders touted the program as one that might prepare "young ministers to better understand the way of life of the people with whom they work."[xl]

UCC students were involved in missionary work throughout South Texas and the state. Several UCC students and graduates would go on to begin or pastor existing churches. Examples include Charles Gaines in Banquete, Roby Goff in Lane City, James West in Ebony Acres, and Jake Setser at College Point Church as a mission of First Baptist Church of Palacios. The UCC choir was also an ambassador for the university, performing at several venues across the state including the annual meeting of the BGCT. UCC students would assist in the construction of missions and churches.[xli]

In the first few years of operation, UCC courses were taught in multiple locations. A separate teaching site for a nursing program at Valley Baptist Hospital in Harlingen began in fall of 1947 under the direction of UCC. The program would ultimately not endure, closing in the spring of 1950. An evening school designed for professionals was conducted in leased space in Downtown Corpus Christi beginning in 1950. Course scheduling would allow a student to earn up to nine hours per semester while working full-time. Offerings also included non-credit instruction and were tailored for students who worked in the area.[xlii]

First Cohort of UCC Nursing Students at Valley Baptist Hospital 1948
1948 Silver King. Special Collections and Archives, Mary and Jeff Bell Library, Texas A&M University-Corpus Christi

As for Cuddihy Field, the City of Corpus Christi began leasing the site from the U.S. Navy in 1947 for use as a general aviation civilian airport. This airport would supplement the Cliff Maus Municipal Airport which had opened in 1928 which lacked sufficient hanger space. The site would allow the city to offer recreational activities for citizens while leasing other buildings for a variety of uses including housing and event space. Corpus Christi Junior College (re-named Del Mar College in 1948)[xliii] leased one of the swimming pools. A drive-in theater would open on August 30, 1947. During the semester that UCC occupied Cuddihy Field, these other activities continued. UCC utilized eight buildings with a lease that was understood by both parties to be temporary. With the many different activities and interests represented at the former base, it would have been a lively place to attend classes.[xliv]

In 1960, Corpus Christi International Airport would open not far from Cuddihy Field. General aviation from Cuddihy Field and commercial service from Cliff Maus Municipal Airport would be moved to this newly constructed facility, ending flight service at both of the older airports. In 1970, the northern portion of Cliff Maus Municipal Airport, located on Airport Road, became the site of the Corpus Christi State School. This is one of 13 state operated facilities for intellectually challenged individuals in Texas. The southern portion of the site is mostly city-owned parkland and recreational areas.

Little evidence of Cuddihy Field remains today. The main runways are no longer discernable, and the site largely remains undeveloped, used for farming, or for small scale industrial activity. The fence surrounding the former military base is largely intact yet overgrown and runs along Old Brownsville Road south of Saratoga Boulevard (Highway 357) just outside the Corpus Christi city limits. A few of the old structures, such as the hangars, remain but are heavily decayed and no longer in use.

Ward Island

As classes began at Cuddihy Field, preparations for a more permanent site were being made. The 223-acre Ward Island would become the third and final site for UCC.[xlv] Serving as an intermediary, the City of Corpus Christi would provide a contract for a 20-year lease to UCC.[xlvi] As with Chase and Cuddihy Fields, Ward Island had former naval facilities that were suitable for on-campus residences, classroom space, and support services. A masonry building that had been the radio school's administration building would serve the same purpose for UCC and be called by the nickname "the shingle." There were two swimming pools which the Baptists would designate one for each gender and separate them by a fence to prevent the mixing of men and women. During a 1948 meeting, the UCC Ministerial Alliance student group discussed a motion to prohibit "mixed bathing" between genders in the pools. The fence remained until 1955.

Barracks were remodeled into student housing and faculty apartments. There were also dining facilities and a gymnasium. As with the other sites, many of these buildings were built hastily and intended only to be temporary structures. Early additions to the campus included an outdoor theatre and designation of a building as a music hall.[xlvii]

First University of Corpus Christi Administration Building, Formerly Naval Administration Building (circa 1948)
Special Collections and Archives, Mary and Jeff Bell Library, Texas A&M University-Corpus Christi.

The interim years since naval occupation and the harsh climate had aged the structures. The cost of maintaining the property was high. Early reports to the Baptist General Convention of Texas indicate these costs, and the lack of outright ownership of the property, led UCC leaders to consider other potential sites in Corpus Christi after securing the Ward Island agreement.[xlviii]

UCC administrators also understood the need to make the campus more inviting as the utilitarian nature of a military base made for rather drab surroundings. However, the natural beauty and unique nature of the campus have always been notable. In a 1949 report to the BGCT, UCC leaders note "This is the only location, as far as we can learn, where a four-year college campus faces out directly on a beautiful bay, and the Gulf of Mexico."[xlix] UCC would expend considerable resources on refurbishment and maintenance of the structures to ready them for a spring 1948 campus opening on Ward Island. As such, the move from Cuddihy Field would be completed over the winter break.[l]

The work to convert a former military base to a university campus would begin in earnest. More colorful and inviting paint schemes were introduced with much of the aesthetics being draw from its geographic location as an island. Additionally, the first library was named after Aubria A. Sanders and an oil portrait placed in the building in his honor.[li] Though the pre-war goat herd would unfortunately not return, through the 1950s around 200 hogs roamed the campus. These were raised and slaughtered to help feed UCC students.[lii]

Leadership

A Board of Trustees had authority over UCC. In 1948, the board had 24 members mostly from South Texas but with several being from Houston. Board members were to serve three-year terms. Mrs. Guy Warren and H. E. Butt Sr. were founding members who served for many years and became significant financial supporters of UCC.[liii]

UCC would ultimately have six presidents with Rev. Hutcherson serving as the first. While the reasons for his resignation are not directly stated, Hutcherson indicated in a letter to faculty that the difficulty in operating UCC and a lack of clarity in its mission perhaps contributed to his decision. These same issues would plague the UCC presidents who followed. Upon receiving Hutcherson's resignation, the UCC board voted unanimously to request he reconsider--to no avail. The board was forced to find a new president for UCC's second year.[liv]

In the interim, a committee of UCC administrators would run operations with John Cobb serving as Chairman of the Religion Department, acting Dean, and acting President. The committee formed to select a new president chose Cavness, who had resigned as Dean in 1947. He would begin his duties on September 8, 1948.[lv]

Raymond McCarey Cavness (1904-1975) was previously an assistant professor of Spanish at Southwest Texas State Teachers College and later President of San Marcos Baptist Academy. At this time, he was one of the youngest university presidents in the nation. He had also been an instructor and graduate student at The University of Texas at Austin earning a Master of Arts and PhD. Prior to his career in higher education, Cavness had been a public-school teacher and superintendent. Cavness served as a Lieutenant Commander on the staff of General Douglas McArthur during World War II and the subsequent military occupation of Japan.[lvi]

As UCC President Cavness was paid $8,000 per year and provided with on campus housing in the house formerly occupied by the station commander. Cavness would prove a capable administrator, but the financial situation of UCC made operations difficult. Cavness would resign in June 1951 to continue his studies at The University of Texas (Austin) and to attend to his health. His resignation would come as a shock to the UCC community.[lvii]

Cavness would become the sixth President of San Angelo College in 1954 where he led the transition of a two-year college into a four year institution named Angelo State University. Cavness dropped the "San" portion of the original name to ensure that in any alphabetical listing of Texas universities, the school would be at the top. He felt this could be an advantage when state legislators were looking over appropriations bills. Following a heart attack in 1965, he retired in 1967. Cavness died on April 11, 1975. The Science Building at ASU is named in his honor.[lviii][lix]

Following the departure of Cavness, Dean A. M. Witherington would serve as interim president for one year until a permanent appointment could be made. Witherington joined the institution in 1949 after serving as department chair and then Dean of Ouachita College in Arkadelphia, Arkansas for 15 years. His experience also included stints as a public-school principal and superintendent in Tennessee and Kentucky. Witherington would resign as UCC Dean in 1953.[lx]

During this same period, the first talk of a merger occurred for the Island University. A proposal to merge another BGCT school, Mary Hardin-Baylor University, located in Belton, with UCC was discussed. At the time, the all-female, Mary Hardin-Baylor was experiencing steep declines in enrollment. Merger plans did not advance beyond these initial discussions yet efficiencies across the BGCT universities would be a consideration for decades.[lxi]

In April 1952, the board named Walter A. Miller to serve as president. Miller had served as superintendent of Odessa, Texas public schools and Dean of Odessa Junior College. He had studied at the University of North Texas, The University of Texas (Austin), and Columbia University. He would remain in the position for 13 years, the longest of any of the UCC presidents. Miller resigned to become superintendent of schools for Crane, Texas in fall of 1965 before retiring in 1972. Walter Miller Hall at UCC was dedicated in his name.[lxii][lxiii]

Dr. Joseph C. Clapp, Jr. would be named UCC president after serving as Vice-President of Development. In that role he had overseen fundraising, recruitment, and public relations building important relationships for UCC. Clapp held a B.A., M.A., and Ph.D. from New Orleans Theological Seminary. He was named interim president upon the departure of Miller.

W.A. Miller Hall (Men's Dormitory) (n.d.)
Special Collections and Archives, Mary and Jeff Bell Library, Texas A&M University-Corpus Christi

Clapp would renew efforts to seek regional accreditation, trim the athletics program, begin a capital campaign, and push to increase faculty salaries to attract more qualified individuals. As Clapp took over as president, he noted that UCC was open to all students, not just Baptists or those who wanted to become ministers. Clapp would pass away during his tenure as president from a heart attack on January 10, 1968.[lxiv][lxv]

In August 1968, Leonard L. Holloway (1923-2003) would be named president. Holloway held a master's degree from the University of Oklahoma and came to UCC after having served as vice president at New Orleans Baptist Theological Seminary and Southern Baptist Theological Seminary in Louisville, Kentucky. He had also been a vice president for the H. E. Butt Foundation. His most recent position was at Mary Hardin-Baylor, a sister school of UCC.[lxvi][lxvii]

UCC President Leonard L. Holloway

Special Collections and Archives, Mary and Jeff Bell Library, Texas A&M University-Corpus Christi

In contrast to Clapp's statement that UCC was open to all, Holloway was disappointed in the high percentage of non-Baptist students at UCC. He hoped to further the ministerial mission of UCC by converting students to become Baptists and opened the Center for Applied Christianity as a research and study center. His presidency was particularly short, as he served only until the following January, or roughly one semester. Holloway would later serve as President of Mary Hardin-Baylor in Belton, a two term Mayor of Kerrville, Texas (1989-1992), and Executive Director of the Kerrville Chamber of Commerce.[lxviii][lxix]

The last president of UCC was Kenneth A. Maroney (1929-2016). He was College Dean and had served as acting president for much of 1968 upon the death of President Clapp. He was again named interim president upon the resignation of Holloway and offered the position on a permanent basis in June 1969.

Maroney was a UCC alumnus who competed on the 1949-1950 basketball team before beginning a long career on the Island University. That year, the Tarpons Basketball team ended the season with an unequaled 25-1 record. Maroney was hired as an instructor and assistant basketball coach in 1957. As a coach, he helped shaped the lives of countless students with many considering him "like family." He later served as Dean of Students and Professor of Psychology. Maroney earned an Ed.D. in Counseling and Professional Administration from North Texas State University in 1962.

Maroney would serve as president through the transition of UCC to a public institution and was given an honorary doctorate degree during UCC's last spring commencement. Maroney would serve on the faculty of Corpus Christi State University until his retirement. He remained active as a supporter of the Tarpon Foundation, Alumni Association, and Islander athletics, being named to the Islander Athletic Hall of Honor in 2002.[lxx][lxxi][lxxii]

UCC President
Kenneth A. Maroney
Special Collections and Archives, Mary and Jeff Bell Library, Texas A&M University-Corpus Christi

Maroney's brother, Robert (Bob) Maroney, was also a standout athlete, coach, and professor over the course of five decades at the Island University. On his retirement in 2007, Dr. Bob Maroney was named Professor Emeritus of the College of Education of Texas A&M University-Corpus Christi by the Texas A&M University System.[lxxiii]

Challenges

A similarly disjointed arrangement for ownership of Ward Island existed as had existed as had been in place at Chase Field in Beeville. The City of Corpus Christi acted as an intermediary between the highly bureaucratic federal government, through the Department of the Navy, and UCC. However, the City of Corpus Christi proved more effective and willing to serve in this capacity than the City of Beeville had been in 1947.

The partnership led to a more productive, albeit still clunky, governance structure. However, UCC, with the help of the city, secured the purchase of Ward Island in 1951. The transfer of ownership required several approvals with most being from various military branches to ensure that the property was not needed for any military purpose in the foreseeable future. This process was slowed by the Korean conflict as the need for military installations again increased during this period. The purchase price for the property was $570,000 with half covered by the BGCT and half to be paid back to the BGCT through a long-term financial campaign undertaken by UCC.[lxxiv][lxxv][lxxvi]

Ownership of the property meant that the university could make extensive changes to the campus without gaining any approvals from the Department of the Navy. At the time of the deed transfer, there were 40 major buildings. Once UCC owned Ward Island, removal of exterior fencing and other structures formerly used by the military would give the campus a more inviting feel. Ownership also allowed for continued renovation and removal of aging naval buildings and infrastructure to occur. Facility maintenance often proved to be a costly undertaking given the poor condition of the infrastructure and the harsh climate.[lxxvii]

Hurricane Carla caused significant damage to the campus when it struck in September 1961. The storm washed out the west entrance from Ocean Drive leaving students to enter through the south gate of the nearby Naval Air Station, drive through the installation, and arrive to campus through the east entrance. The storm led to a decline in student enrollment and contributed to a financial burden not only in lost revenue but due to costly campus reparations.[lxxviii]

From its founding, UCC sought to gain regional accreditation. This was important for students to be able to transfer their earned credits to other universities as well as to have their degrees carry a higher distinction for quality. In addressing the campus ownership issue, university leaders took the first of many necessary steps towards this goal.[lxxix] However, accreditation would prove a long and difficult undertaking.

Broadly speaking, accreditation concerns not only the governance and quality of academic programs but also the support students receive in other areas of the university as well. Impediments were present on numerous fronts. In the earliest years, many faculty members lacked the higher level of academic degree required for regional accreditation. Efforts to hire faculty with terminal degrees (e.g., Ph.D.) proved difficult. This issue was addressed over time but attracting faculty remained an ongoing challenge in part due to low salaries.[lxxx] UCC also preferred that faculty be Baptists or at least Protestant. In the 1961 report to the BGCT, President M. A. Miller noted that the percentage of faculty identifying as Baptists had been increased and "if a Baptist cannot be found for the position, the next step is to know they are Christian and members of an evangelical Protestant group" in his description of faculty recruitment efforts.[lxxxi]

The number of degree programs offered was often too great for the number of students enrolled at UCC. This situation led to concerns over the quality of instruction. Fifteen years after its founding, the university had programs in English, biology, chemistry, Bible, history, mathematics, Spanish, speech, education, music, art, sociology, French, physics, government, and geology.[lxxxii]

Accreditors assessed many of the old naval buildings to be substandard and subject to fire due to their wooden construction. This was a justifiable concern as a wooden structure building used for education classroom space caught fire in 1958 and was a complete loss. An additional concern was the ability of the structures to withstand the storms that were a regular occurrence on the bay front location. This point would also prove valid as a major hurricane would strike the campus in 1970 causing extensive damage to the wooden structures.[lxxxiii]

For many of the early years of UCC, the library had inadequate holdings to support the student body and academic programs. This issue was addressed with the addition of a new library building on campus in 1963.

This structure is still affectionately known as the "round building" and was a modern, state of the art building at the time of its construction. The 24,000-square-foot building cost $300,000 with space for 80,000 volumes. The new library was a gift of the Butt Foundation.[lxxxiv] Mary Elizabeth Holdsworth Butt (1903-1993) was instrumental in bringing this building to campus and supplementing the library's collection.[lxxxv] She was a philanthropist and early backer of UCC along with her husband, Howard E. Butt, Sr.

The library holdings increased greatly from just over 13,000 in 1955 to 57,000 in 1969, helping address a deficiency that was hampering accreditation.[lxxxvi] As with the round building, many of the masonry buildings built by UCC remain in use today as most have been repurposed for other functions than originally constructed.[lxxxvii]

Construction of the University of Corpus Christi Library (circa 1963)
Special Collections and Archives, Mary and Jeff Bell Library, Texas A&M University-Corpus Christi

Building a University

In the 1950s, UCC began to develop its own identity as it was no longer a tenant of the U.S. Navy. Ownership of the land and a desire for accreditation led university administrators to develop a master plan for the campus in 1952. One year later, the Nueces County Commissioners Court officially changed the name of Ward Island to University Heights to recognize the prominent place of UCC in the community. This change was requested by UCC officials.

Long-time Corpus Christi historian and columnist Murphy Givens noted the humor in this name as the island is "flat as a floor." However, this official change did not take hold and use of the name Ward Island remains prevalent. In this same year, the long-standing tradition of giving buildings nautical themed names began.[lxxxviii][lxxxix][xc]

University of Corpus Christi Entrance Sign (1947)
Special Collections and Archives, Mary and Jeff Bell Library, Texas A&M University-Corpus Christi

Construction of the university's first brick building was begun in January 1955. The $150,000 structure was named after Gazzie Warren, an early supporter and board member of UCC. Warren Hall was 18,700 square feet and would accommodate 84 female students.[xci]

Residence Hall (Formerly Warren Hall) at CCSU (1979)
Alumni Update, June 1979. Special Collections and Archives, Mary and Jeff Bell Library,
Texas A&M University-Corpus Christi

A new $100,000 administration building was completed in 1956. The building was constructed behind the Navy's old administration building and consisted of a one-story, 8,200-square-foot air-conditioned building.[xcii] W. A. Miller Hall was built in 1957 as a dormitory to house 100 male students and still stands on the campus having been re-named "Classroom East." The Science Building was built the following year and is now named "Classroom West."

In 1967, the red brick Glasscock Memorial Student Union Building was dedicated. Mr. Charles Gus Glasscock (1895-1965)[xciii] served as an early board member of UCC and university supporter. The facility included a dining facility, chapel, and the UCC student center. The Glasscock Building is now home to the student success center. The small chapel remains part of the building to the present.

The Moody/Sustainers Field House was donated by the Moody Foundation and the Sustainer's Club of Corpus Christi with each group contributing $100,000. Guy Warren led this fundraising effort for the Sustainers. [xciv]

Glasscock Student Success Center (2020)
Andrew Johnson

Classroom West (2020)
Andrew Johnson

In addition to the start of many construction projects and physical changes to the campus, programmatic changes occurred during this time as well. Teacher education has been a popular major since the earliest years of the Island University. Beginning in 1952, a kindergarten was started on the Island within the Division of Teacher Training.[xcv] The program was expanded to include additional grades and programs such as special education. At the time of implementation, the special education program for teacher training was the only specialized program in the State of Texas.

In 1954, a petroleum engineering school was established through contributions from companies in the energy industry to help supply the demand for engineers in the bourgeoning South Texas energy sector. Mr. Norman Lamont was recruited from Texas Technological College to lead this program.[xcvi][xcvii] The petroleum program would not be a lasting addition to the curriculum but would emphasize the breadth of offerings even at a time when enrollments would not support the number of degrees offered. UCC enrollment reached a high-water mark of 996 in 1967.[xcviii]

In 1957, the Department of Marine Sciences was added. This would mark the beginning of work in an area for which the Island University would become world-renowned. Early reports for the department note that research work was conducted on the Laguna Madre areas of Texas in support of fishing and sports industries.[xcix] The U.S. Geological Survey would open an office on Ward Island in partnership with UCC for the study of the Gulf of Mexico and the Caribbean in 1969.[c]

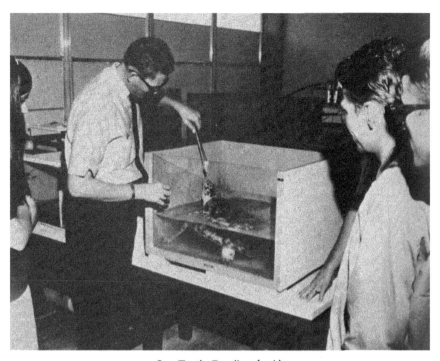

Sea Turtle Feeding (n.d.)
Special Collections and Archives, Mary and Jeff Bell Library, Texas A&M University-Corpus Christi

Struggles

In 1961, UCC almost lost its Texas Education Agency (TEA) teacher certification accreditation. The TEA certification is separate from regional accreditation but critical as it is required for graduates to be able to obtain a teaching certification in Texas. Teacher education was a popular major, and the loss could have led to one-third of the student body not being able to pursue teacher certification upon completion of their degree. While UCC was able to appeal the decision and take steps to remedy the situation, the case highlighted the strain the university faced in its ability to deliver programs. This accreditation issue was but one aspect of the larger challenge that gaining regional accreditation posed for the entire university. UCC would gain full accreditation from the regional accreditation body in 1968, over 20 years after its founding.[ci]

Highly related to the struggle for accreditation were the ongoing financial strains UCC faced. While the BGCT provided an annual allocation to fund operations, it was far from enough. In 1966, it was noted that the cost of upkeep for the campus was an excessive portion of the budget.[cii] Further, BGCT supported ministerial students through scholarships. These funds were not a direct appropriation but instead covered tuition and fees for the student. In turn, the university had to provide the educational services for these students. Evidence suggests that the BGCT struggled to provide adequate funding for its nine universities. In 1955, an emergency five-year $12 million campaign was established to assist all BGCT universities.[ciii]

Some of these funds would be gained through church offerings. UCC consistently relied on fundraising and local supporters, particularly board members, to maintain operations. Indeed, bills were often past due and loans were necessary to complete several academic years. Tuition for a small private university was already expensive, leaving little ability to raise rates which would have simultaneously served to dissuade students from attending due to cost.[civ]

Many challenges highlighted through the accreditation process were not solved but rather limited. These challenges were exacerbated when Hurricane Celia struck Corpus Christi on August 3, 1970. The storm had winds up to 118 miles per hour with the center of the storm hitting nearby Port Aransas to the north of campus. The storm was one of the worst to hit Corpus Christi in recorded history. It was devastating in terms of property damage to the city and the UCC campus. UCC Dean Wrotenbery indicated virtually every roof on campus had damage, the library sustained considerable damage to its collection, and several of the naval buildings as well as the auditorium were a complete loss.[cv]

Damage to the UCC Library Caused by Hurricane Celia (1970)
Special Collections and Archives, Mary and Jeff Bell Library, Texas A&M University-Corpus Christi

Dr. Richard Marcum and Dr. Carl Wrotenbery Survey Damaged Books in the Library Following Hurricane Celia
Special Collections and Archives, Mary and Jeff Bell Library, Texas A&M University-Corpus Christi

Damage Caused by Hurricane Celia to Campus Housing (1970)
Special Collections and Archives, Mary and Jeff Bell Library, Texas A&M University-Corpus Christi

Following Hurricane Celia, a disagreement over the funding of repairs to the campus between the BGCT, the UCC board, and campus administration ensued. Emergency funding was necessary to prepare the campus to open the following month for the fall 1970 semester. The main sticking point was the UCC board's decision to use federal relief funds to make repairs as insurance payments were slow to materialize. [cvi]

The BGCT had been unwilling to provide any immediate financial assistance to UCC in the wake of the hurricane.[cvii] To fill the immediate need for funding, UCC had sought and received a $500,000 Small Business Administration loan as a line of credit while insurance claims were negotiated.[cviii][cix]

There was a strong sentiment that the use of this federal funding violated the separation of church and state which many BGCT delegates believed should have been respected without exception. Reporting in the *Dallas Morning News* framed the situation in stark terms stating "BCGT told the school to repay the loan with money borrowed from an agency other than the federal government or withdraw from the denomination."[cx] Further, UCC supporter Howard E. Butt, Jr. held this same sentiment viewing the use of government funds as improper.[cxi]

The rift over how to finance the campus rebuilding was the latest in a succession of disappointments in the eyes of many BGCT members. UCC had never grown its enrollment to levels that the BGCT expected or that would enable the university to operate with financial security. Other BGCT-sponsored universities were increasing enrollments and, perhaps more importantly to members, had larger enrollments in ministerial education programs. Creating additional challenges to enrollment, the BGCT opened Dallas Baptist University and Houston Baptist University in the mid-1960s thus creating additional competition for prospective students.[cxii]

Gains in enrollment at UCC had been difficult to achieve by merely recruiting from South Texas. Recruitment efforts aimed at New York and Chicago had yielded the increased numbers that administrators desired but many of these students had no interest in studying for the ministry. Indeed, these students were typically from well-off families that could afford to pay the private school tuition. The students were much more interested in a liberal arts experience than starting churches or becoming members of the clergy.[cxiii]

Corpus Christi was supportive of UCC; however, the mission of UCC was sometimes at odds with the needs of the community. For instance, the BGCT required its board members to be Baptists, thus restricting many willing and capable leaders from the local community from serving in this capacity. Across the state, decreasing church membership, fewer churches being founded, and diminishing funds were leading the BGCT to re-evaluate its sponsorship of universities. The BGCT released control over Baylor Medical School in Houston in 1969 and in the following year released Baylor Dental School in Dallas.[cxiv]

The BGCT tracked the religious affiliation of students at its affiliated universities, and UCC consistently disappointed in this regard. The BGCT wanted a large percentage of the student body, and preferably the faculty, to be Baptist. Achieving the desired homogeneity in the student body was difficult in South Texas given the large number of Catholics in the area.[cxv]

Christopher College, a Catholic-supported institution, operated in Corpus Christi from 1957 to 1968. It was located on Saratoga Boulevard between Airline Road and South Staples Street.[cxvi] This institution was founded as Mary Immaculate Teacher Training Institute and changed its name to Christopher College in 1965 when reorganized as a junior college. While the college also struggled financially, during its rather brief existence the institution represented additional local competition for UCC.[cxvii]

Diverging interests in student recruitment was nothing new as these efforts had long been challenging for administrators and were ultimately disappointing for the BGCT. In the early days of UCC, the demand for education was very high given the post-war boom. Nearby schools, such as the Texas College of Arts & Industries (Kingsville), were experiencing record enrollments.[cxviii] The newness of UCC, its core focus on the ministry, and its higher cost of attendance likely pushed many prospective students to other universities. Later, the out of state recruitment efforts yielded few Baptists and ministerial students but rather diversified the religious affiliation found on campus and drove demand for majors other than religious studies. When enrollments did increase, it was more a result of this out of state influx than an increase in educational opportunity for the local population. The end of the World War II era G.I. Bill and the higher tuition rates at a private school made education at UCC less attainable, especially for lower socio-economic people. The number of Hispanic students at UCC was low relative to the demographics of the South Texas region. In 1950, university administration reported 35 Latin American students out of a total student population of 556. This year did mark the first year that international students would attend UCC with one student each from Mexico and Chile. By 1956, students from 13 foreign countries, 12 states, and 77 Texas counties were part of the student body. [cxix]

UCC's challenges contributed to a push for a state sponsored university to be in Corpus Christi. Even in the early 1950s, state and local leaders recognized the limitations of UCC to fulfill the educational needs of the region. The cost of attendance and sense of exclusion for many due to its Baptist affiliation, made UCC a less desirable option for some South Texans. Additionally, there was a concern that many students could not afford to or would not travel far for their education. Efforts were sought to address this situation. A legislative proposal by Corpus

Christi State Representative William H. Shireman in 1953 would have made Del Mar College in Corpus Christi into a four-year college along with two similarly situated junior colleges in the state. While the measure did not pass the Texas Legislature, the concerns over educational access in the region were present even in the early days of UCC.[cxx]

By the 1970s, Corpus Christi was the largest city in Texas without a state-sponsored senior level university as San Antonio had secured construction of a University of Texas affiliated campus in the late 1960s.[cxxi] The business community in Corpus Christi also recognized that economic development may be hampered by the lack of a comprehensive public institution. The Chamber of Commerce formed a committee to study the issue in late 1966.[cxxii] By 1968, the Coordinating Board of the Texas College and University System determined that an upper-level university was needed in Corpus Christi.[cxxiii] A citizens group led by John Crutchfield (1919-2011) also championed the cause.[cxxiv][cxxv] Crutchfield was an influential Corpus Christi businessman as an owner of a petroleum engineering consulting firm, Crutchfield & Pruett.[cxxvi][cxxvii]

During this same period, the BGCT was taking actions that would position UCC to become independent from the convention and thus able to be brought under control of the State of Texas. However, this was not a universally popular idea. Much of the final push towards independence on the part of the BGCT rested on the Carden Report which the convention had commissioned. Dr. William R. Carden, Jr., (1937-2018) a former administrator at Stetson University in Florida, was contracted and charged with studying the financial situation of all nine of the BGCT-affiliated universities. The report he submitted recommended that UCC be released from BGCT control effectively letting it work towards transfer to the state. The report also recommended that the BGCT close Howard Payne College and Wayland Baptist College. For the state's part, there was also discussion at the time over the need for state-supported universities in these areas, similar to the situation in Corpus Christi. However, the state ultimately did not act in these other cases, and these schools were ultimately not closed. Howard Payne University and Wayland Baptist University remain affiliated with the BGCT.[cxxviii] Other recommendations dealing with organizational changes and finances were also made by Carden. The report concluded that half of the BGCT universities did not have sufficient library resources and recommended that some "non-Baptists" be allowed to serve on the UCC board. Ultimately, a committee of 12 BGCT members reviewed the report and recommended action on the items pertaining to UCC.

Carden would go on to work for his alma mater Baylor University, as a banker at several banks in Texas, and as founder of the Center for Banking and Financial Studies in the Baylor Business School in 1982. His professional life was capped by board membership of KFC Corporation and the financial company Q2. [cxxix][cxxx]

The Carden report and subsequent recommendations were not without controversy and were not embraced by some affiliated with UCC. President Holloway responded to a news story about the potential for UCC to separate from the BGCT by stating that he was not interested in the idea. Holloway would leave UCC in 1969 just as the recommendations of the Carden report were being considered. UCC Board Chairman Othal Brand of McAllen was more direct in his opposition to allowing UCC to become independent stating in early 1969, "As long as I am a member of the board, it will be a Baptist school."[cxxxi] Brand noted the recent progress made in increased enrollment and campus building projects. UCC had also been successful in obtaining full regional accreditation in 1967.[cxxxii]

In the end, many reasons contributed to perhaps an understanding or at least inevitability that the UCC model was not sustainable. The aftermath of Hurricane Celia accelerated the already diverging trajectories of the BGCT and UCC.

The Island University was to rebuild its mission and its physical campus from Hurricane Celia to become an upper-level public institution that would serve a more broad, diverse, and larger study body. UCC was an attractive candidate for acquisition by the state as opposed to creating a new public university from the ground up. UCC leaders knew the addition of a state university in Corpus Christi would have competed for students, likely further contributing to the ongoing enrollment and financial struggles. Actions by the UCC governing board worked to ensure that UCC transitioned to become a state-supported campus. On January 21, 1971, the UCC board acted to become independent of the BGCT while selecting Corpus Christi Mayor Jack R. Blackmon (1918-2006) as its Chairman[cxxxiii]. This move would underscore the increased reliance on the City of Corpus Christi and the community as partners of the university as support of the BGCT would fully diminish by 1973. The board would be instrumental in this transitional period.[cxxxiv]

The BGCT would end its affiliation with UCC with initial action on March 9, 1971 and adoption by a vote of all BGCT delegates in October of that year. A two-year transition period was implemented to allow many students to complete their studies and for an orderly conversion to state control.[cxxxv] UCC held its final commencement ceremony in summer of 1973. In 26 years, UCC graduated over 1,500 students and set the foundation for higher education on Ward Island and in the Coastal Bend region. The university that started as UCC would continue and grow during a new phase beginning in the fall of 1973.[cxxxvi]

President Dr. Kenneth Maroney Award the Last UCC Degree to Susie Austin (Haisler). Also Pictured is UCC Dean Dr. Carl Wrotenbery
Original Photograph by George Tuley (1973) Special Collections and Archives, Mary and Jeff Bell Library, Texas A&M University-Corpus Christi

Christian Education Activities Corporation

An impediment felt by some BGCT members, community leader Charles H. Butt, Jr., and the Corpus Christi Baptist Association Mission Superintendent Dr. W. H. Colson was the abandonment of the religious mission of UCC should it become a state institution. Even through the financial struggles, educating ministers and its missionary work in South Texas were deeply important to these stakeholders. In the negotiations, a compromise was forged to allow for land and financial resources be set apart to further this mission of UCC. Howard Butt,

Jr. was instrumental in ensuring that ten acres on Ward Island be set aside from the transfer of property to be used for Christian educational studies. The Christian Education Activities Corporation (CEAC) was founded to serve as the legal successor to UCC. In this capacity, the organization would receive control over the one and a half million-dollar endowment that UCC had in place for religious studies.[cxxxvii][cxxxviii]

The UCC board transitioned to become the first CEAC board. They were charged with continuing the mission of Christian studies in South Texas. Theology courses were offered beginning in 1977, taught mostly by HPU Associate Professor Dr. Kenneth Bradshaw (1929-2013). Students at CCSU could also take the courses on religion as electives.[cxxxix] The Baptist Learning Center of South Texas (BLC) was established in 1980 on Ward Island. The student body of BLC was largely Baptist, and the curriculum was focused on religious studies. Coursework was offered by Corpus Christi State University, Howard Payne University, and the BLC. A partnership with Howard Payne University allowed for degrees to be conferred.[cxl][cxli]

In 1997, the BLC added a Master of Divinity degree to the offerings on Ward Island through a partnership with another BGCT affiliated University, Hardin-Simmons University of Abilene.[cxlii] In 2005, the Bill and Doris Stark Conference Center opened with four apartments to provide housing for faculty and a meeting

Construction of the Christian Learning Center (1980)

Alumni Update, June 1980. Special Collections and Archives, Mary and Jeff Bell Library, Texas A&M University-Corpus Christi

room. In 2004, the BLC name was changed to the South Texas School of Christian Studies and later to Stark College and Seminary. This center remains devoted to Christian studies at its location on the eastern part of Ward Island and has sites in McAllen, Victoria, and San Antonio. Stark College continues the religious mission of UCC.[cxliii]

Stark College on Ward Island (2020)
Andrew Johnson

References

[i] Wrotenbery, R. (1998). Baptist Island College. Fort Worth, Texas: Eakin Press.

[ii] Russell, M. & Murray, L. S. Baylor University. Handbook of Texas Online. Texas State Historical Association. https://www.tshaon line.org/handbook/entries/baylor-university

[iii] Wrotenbery, C. R. (1998). Baptist Island College. Fort Worth, Texas: Eakin

[iv] Celelli, T. (2012). Missions through education: The continuing legacy of the University of Corpus Christi and the South Texas School of Christian Studies. In M. E. Williams, Texas Baptist History (pp. 69-80). Texas Baptist Historical Society.

[v] Wrotenbery, C. R. (1998). Baptist Island College. Fort Worth, Texas: Eakin Press.

[vi] Wrotenbery, C. R. (1998). Baptist Island College. Fort Worth, Texas: Eakin Press.

[vii] Celelli, T. (2012). Missions through education: The continuing legacy of the University of Corpus Christi and the South Texas School of Christian Studies. In M. E. Williams, Texas Baptist History (pp. 69-80). Texas Baptist Historical Society.

[viii] Wrotenbery, C. R. (1998). Baptist Island College. Fort Worth, Texas: Eakin

[ix] Wrotenbery, C. R. (1998). Baptist Island College. Fort Worth, Texas: Eakin

[x] Wrotenbery, C. R. (1998). Baptist Island College. Fort Worth, Texas: Eakin

[xi] Delaney, C. (2013, May). Corpus Christi's 'University of the Air'. U.S. Naval Institute. https://www.usni.org/magazines/naval-his tory-magazine/2013/may/corpus-christis-university-air

[xii] Wrotenbery, C. R. (1998). Baptist Island College. Fort Worth, Texas: Eakin

[xiii] Ehrlich, A. (2021, February 3). NAS-Chase Field trained pilots for nearly 50 years. Corpus Christi Caller-Times. https://www.caller.com/story/news/special-reports/building-our-future/throwback/2021/02/03/nas-chase-field-trained-pilots nearly-50-years/4350311001/

[xiv] Wrotenbery, C. R. (1998). Baptist Island College. Fort Worth, Texas: Eakin

[xv] University of Corpus Christi plans huge expansion (1953, June 7). Dallas Morning News.

[xvi] Kreneck, H., Gammage, B., & Paschal, S. (2007). Texas A&M University-Corpus Christi: The Island University: 60 years, 1947-2007. Texas A&M University-Corpus Christi: Texas A&M University-Corpus Christi: Division of Institutional Advancement.

[xvii] Branning, (1989, January 12). Baptist opened university. Corpus Christi Caller-Times, p. 67.

[xviii] Wrotenbery, R. (1998). Baptist Island College. Fort Worth, Texas: Eakin Press.

[xix] Celelli, T. (2012). Missions through education: The continuing legacy of the University of Corpus Christi and the South Texas School of Christian Studies. In M. E. Williams, Texas Baptist History (pp. 69-80). Texas Baptist Historical

[xx] Wrotenbery, C. R. (1998). Baptist Island College. Fort Worth, Texas: Eakin

[xxi] Sanders library to occupy site of Navy Library. (1947, June 8). Corpus Christi Caller-Times, 18.

[xxii] Branning, C. (1989, January 12). Baptist opened university. Corpus Christi Caller-Times, 67.

[xxiii] Wrotenbery, C. R. (1998). Baptist Island College. Fort Worth, Texas: Eakin

[xxiv] Wrotenbery, C. R. (1998). Baptist Island College. Fort Worth, Texas: Eakin

[xxv] Kreneck, T. , Gammage, B., & Paschal, S. (2007). Texas A&M University-Corpus Christi: The Island University: 60 years,

1947-2007. Texas A&M University-Corpus Christi: Division of Institutional Advancement.

[xxvi] Nelson, (1966, March 27). UCC aims at accreditation. Corpus Christi Caller-Times, p. 15.

[xxvii] Wrotenbery, C. R. (1998). Baptist Island College. Fort Worth, Texas: Eakin

[xxviii] Branning, (1989, January 12). Baptist opened university. Corpus Christi Caller-Times, p. 67.

[xxix] Wrotenbery, C. R. (1998). Baptist Island College. Fort Worth, Texas: Eakin

[xxx] Wrotenbery, C. R. (1998). Baptist Island College. Fort Worth, Texas: Eakin

[xxxi] Chase Field. National Register of Historic Places. https://npgallery.nps.gov/pdfhost/ docs/NRHP/Text/64500646.pdf

[xxxii] Garza (2020, August 22). Texas Department of Criminal Justice. https://www.tdcj.texas.gov/unit_directory/ni.html

[xxxiii] Chase Field (2020, August 22). Texas A&M University-Corpus Christi. https://lsuasc.tamucc.edu/ test-sites/ chase.html

[xxxiv] George Cuddihy. USNA Virtual Memorial Wall. https://usnamemorialhall.org/index.php/GEORGE_T._CUDDIHY,_LT,_USN

[xxxv] Leatherwood, (2010, June 15). Naval Air Station, Corpus Christi. Handbook of Texas Online. Texas State Historical Association. https:// tshaonline.org/handbook/online/articles/qbn01

[xxxvi] Ward Island takes Comet Nine, 7-5. (1947,June 15). Corpus Christi Caller-Times,

[xxxvii] Baptist General Convention of Texas. (1947). Annual of the Baptist General Convention of

[xxxviii] Hunter, C. A., & Hunter, L. G. (2000). Texas A&M University Charleston, SC: Arcadia.

[xxxix] Branning, C. (1989, January 12). Baptist opened university. Corpus Christi Caller-Times, 67.

[xl] Baptist General Convention of Texas. (1956). Annual of the Baptist General Convention of Texas.

[xli] Wrotenbery, C. R. (1998). Baptist Island College. Fort Worth, Texas: Eakin Press.

[xlii] Wrotenbery, C. R. (1998). Baptist Island College. Fort Worth, Texas: Eakin Press.

[xliii] Tijerina, R. (1999, November 28). Education in Corpus Christi: A timeline. Corpus Christi Caller-Times, p. L7.

[xliv] Dodson, A. (1947, October 19). Cuddihy becomes collegiate as Baptist University moves in. The Corpus Christi Caller-Times.

[xlv] Texas Baptists accept contract for Ward Island. (1947, November 26). Corpus Christi Caller and Daily Herald, p. 1.

[xlvi] Branning, C. (1989, January 12). Baptist opened university. Corpus Christi Caller-Times, p. 67.

[xlvii] Wrotenbery, C. R. (1998). Baptist Island College. Fort Worth, Texas: Eakin Press.

[xlviii] Baptist General Convention of Texas. (1948). Annual of the Baptist General Convention of Texas.

[xlix] Baptist General Convention of Texas. (1949). Annual of the Baptist General Convention of Texas.

[l] UCC personnel begin moving to Ward Island. (1947, December 20). Corpus Christi Caller and Daily Herald, p. 24.

[li] Wrotenbery, C. R. (1998). Baptist Island College. Fort Worth, Texas: Eakin Press.

[lii] Rosser, J. (1978, October 12). CCSU worker must move after years on campus. Corpus Christi Caller, p. 66.

[liii] Baptist General Convention of Texas. (1948). Annual of the Baptist General Convention of Texas.

[liv] Wrotenbery, C. R. (1998). Baptist Island College. Fort Worth, Texas: Eakin Press.

[lv] Baptist General Convention of Texas. (1948). Annual of the Baptist General Convention of Texas.

[lvi] Wrotenbery, C. R. (1998). Baptist Island College. Fort Worth, Texas: Eakin Press.

[lvii] Wrotenbery, C. R. (1998). Baptist Island College. Fort Worth, Texas: Eakin Press.

[lviii] Fulton, C. C. (2017, May 12). ASU's first four-year graduates walked 50 years ago. San Angelo Standard-Times.

[lix] Wrotenbery, C. R. (1998). Baptist Island College. Fort Worth, Texas: Eakin Press.

[Ix] Wrotenbery, C. R. (1998). Baptist Island College. Fort Worth, Texas: Eakin Press.

[lxi] Wrotenbery, C. R. (1998). Baptist Island College. Fort Worth, Texas: Eakin Press.

[lxii] Baptist General Convention of Texas. (1952). Annual of the Baptist General Convention of Texas.

[lxiii] Dr. Miller toils to better UCC. (1964, November 4). Corpus Christi Caller-Times, p. 25.

[lxiv] Nelson, G. (1966, March 27). UCC aims at accreditation. Cor pus Christi Caller-Times, p. 15.

[lxv] Wrotenbery, C. R. (1998). Baptist Island College. Fort Worth, Texas: Eakin Press.

[lxvi] Wrotenbery, C. R. (1998). Baptist Island College. Fort Worth, Texas: Eakin Press.

[lxvii] Fernandez, S. L. (2003, August 20). Ex-UCC president dies - Leonard Holloway served here in 1967. Corpus Christi Caller-Times.

[lxviii] Wrotenbery, C. R. (1998). Baptist Island College. Fort Worth, Texas: Eakin Press.

[lxix] Central Texas Obituaries. (2003, August 20). Temple Daily Telegram. https://www.tdtnews.com/archive/article_f606157b- a872-5447-92e9-da73665232da.html

[lxx] UCC alumni to support new A&I-Corpus Christi. (1973, February 11). Corpus Christi Caller-Times., p. 45.

[lxxi] Wrotenbery, C. R. (1998). Baptist Island College. Fort Worth, Texas: Eakin Press.

[lxxii] Hall of Fame. Kenneth Maroney. Texas A&M University Corpus Christi Athletics. https://goislanders.com/hof.aspx?hof=32

[lxxiii] Hall of Fame. Bob Maroney. Texas A&M University-Corpus Christi Athletics. https://goislanders.com/honors/hall-of-honor?hof=8

[lxxiv] Baptist General Convention of Texas. (1950). Annual of the Baptist General Convention of Texas.

[lxxv] Baptist General Convention of Texas. (1951). Annual of the Baptist General Convention of Texas.

[lxxvi] Wrotenbery, C. R. (1998). Baptist Island College. Fort Worth, Texas: Eakin Press.

[lxxvii] Wrotenbery, C. R. (1998). Baptist Island College. Fort Worth, Texas: Eakin Press.

[lxxviii] Bailey bridge to UCC to be removed today. (1962, May 15).Corpus Christi Caller, p. 30.

[lxxix] Wrotenbery, C. R. (1998). Baptist Island College. Fort Worth, Texas: Eakin Press.

[lxxx] Nelson, G. (1966, March 27). UCC aims at accreditation. Corpus Christi Caller-Times, p. 15.

[lxxxi] Baptist General Convention of Texas. (1961). Annual of the Baptist General Convention of Texas.

[lxxxii] Baptist General Convention of Texas. (1962). Annual of the Baptist General Convention of Texas.

[lxxxiii] Wrotenbery, C. R. (1998). Baptist Island College. Fort Worth, Texas: Eakin Press.

[lxxxiv] Enrollment is 600 at UCC this fall. (1964, November 4). Corpus Christi Caller, p. 21.

[lxxxv] Kreneck, T. H., Gammage, B., & Paschal, S. (2007). Texas A&M University-Corpus Christi: The Island University: 60 years, 1947-2007. Texas A&M University-Corpus Christi: Division of Institutional Advancement.

[lxxxvi] Young, N. B. (2020, August 26). Texas A&M University Corpus Christi. Texas State Historical Association Handbook of Texas

Online. https://www.tshaonline.org/handbook/entries/texas-a-m-uni-versity-corpus-christi

[lxxxvii] Wrotenbery, C. R. (1998). Baptist Island College. Fort Worth, Texas: Eakin Press.

[lxxxviii] Givens, M. (2013, February 6). What was the big secret on John Ward's island? Corpus Christi Caller-Times.

[lxxxix] Ward Island is no more; name changed. (1953, May 28). Corpus Christi Caller, p. 47.

[xc] Wrotenbery, C.R. (1998). Baptist Island College. Fort Worth, Texas: Eakin Press.

[xci] Baptist General Convention of Texas. (1956). Annual of the Baptist General Convention of Texas.

[xcii] UCC Administration Building. (1956, February 19). Corpus Christi Caller-Times.

[xciii] Conner, J. E. (n.d.). Glasscock, Charles Gus. Texas State Historical Association Handbook of Texas Online. https://www.tshaon line.org/handbook/entries/glasscock-charles-gus

[xciv] College students are home more. (1968, February 4). Corpus Christi Caller-Times, p. 74.

[xcv] Baptist General Convention of Texas. (1952). Annual of the Baptist General Convention of Texas.

[xcvi] Baptist General Convention of Texas. (1954). Annual of the Baptist General Convention of Texas.

[xcvii] Baptist General Convention of Texas. (1955). Annual of the Baptist General Convention of Texas.

[xcviii] Kreneck, T. H., Gammage, B., & Paschal, S. (2007). Texas A&M University-Corpus Christi: The Island University: 60 years, 1947-2007. Texas A&M University-Corpus Christi: Division of Institutional Advancement.

[xcix] Baptist General Convention of Texas. (1958). Annual of the Baptist General Convention of Texas.

[c] Baptist General Convention of Texas. (1971). Annual of the Baptist General Convention of Texas.

[ci] Wrotenbery, C. R. (1998). Baptist Island College. Fort Worth, Texas: Eakin Press.

[cii] Nelson, G. (1966, March 27). UCC aims at accreditation. Corpus Christi Caller-Times, p. 15.

[ciii] Baptists set offering for 9 colleges. (1955, March 23). Dallas Morning News.

[civ] Wrotenbery, C. R. (1998). Baptist Island College. Fort Worth, Texas: Eakin Press.

[cv] UCC to remain closed until fall; Del Mar will resume. (1970, August 5). Corpus Christi Caller-Times, p. 3.

[cvi] Celelli, T. (2012). Missions through education: The continuing legacy of the University of Corpus Christi and the South Texas School of Christian Studies. In M. E. Williams, Texas Baptist History (pp. 69-80). Texas Baptist Historical Society.

[cvii] Wrotenbery, C. R. (1998). Baptist Island College. Fort Worth, Texas: Eakin Press.

[cviii] Deswysen, E. (1971, January 22). Blackmon selected chairman. Corpus Christi Caller, p. 1.

[cix] Reiste, B. (1983, April 10). Public determination made CCSU succeed. Corpus Christi Caller-Times, p. 1.

[ex] Parmley, H. (1971, March 10). BGCT head opposes 'Church use of State'. Dallas Morning News.

[cxi] Wrotenbery, C. R. (1998). Baptist Island College. Fort Worth, Texas: Eakin Press.

[cxii] Wrotenbery, C. R. (1998). Baptist Island College. Fort Worth, Texas: Eakin Press.

[cxiii] Wrotenbery, C. R. (1998). Baptist Island College. Fort Worth, Texas: Eakin Press.

[cxiv] Parmley, H. (1971, March 10). BGCT head opposes 'Church use of State'. Dallas Morning News.

[cxv] Hunter, C. A., & Hunter, L. G. (2000). Texas A&M University Kingsville. Charleston, SC: Arcadia.

[cxvi] College students are home more. (1968, February 4). Corpus Christi Caller-Times, p. 74.

[cxvii] Christopher College of Corpus Christi. (2020, August 29). Texas State Historical Association Handbook of Texas: https://www.tshaonline.org/handbook/ entries/christopher-college-of corpus-christi

[cxviii] Hunter, C. A., & Hunter, L. G. (2000). Texas A&M University Kingsville. Charleston, SC: Arcadia.

[cxix] Baptist General Convention of Texas. (1956). Annual of the Baptist General Convention of Texas.

[cxx] Morehead, R. M. (1953, March 20). Senate votes to revive college expansion plan. Dallas Morning News.

[cxxi] History of the UT System. (2020, August 23). The University of Texas System. https://www.utsystem.edu/offices/chancellor/ history ut-system

[cxxii] Jackson, R. M. (1972, May 16). The aim is a university of excellence and stature. Corpus Christi Caller, p. 14.

[cxxiii] Hunter, C. A., & Hunter, L. G. (2000). Texas A&M University Kingsville. Charleston, SC: Arcadia.

[cxxiv] Reiste, B. (1983, April 10). Public determination made CCSU succeed. Corpus Christi Caller-Times, p. 1.

[cxxv] Large gifts pace A&I-CC fund drive. (1972, July 4). The Corpus Christi Caller-Times, p. 20.

[cxxvi] John W. Crutchfield. (2011, August 11). Obituary. Austin American-Statesman. https://legcy.co/3qgseYU

[cxxvii] Smith, M. D. (2011, August 11). Oilman, civic leader dies at 92 - Held many leadership roles throughout city. Corpus Christi Caller Times, Bl.

[cxxviii] Texas Baptist college officials rally around schools after re port of closing. (1968, July 4). Corpus Christi Caller-Times, p.8.

[cxxix] Kelly, J. (1968, July 24). Baptist educators hear report on Texas colleges. Dallas Morning News.

[cxxx] William R. Carden, Jr. (2018). OakCrest Funeral Home. https://www.oakcrestwaco.com/memorials/william-r-carden-jr/3685871/

[cxxxi] Opposition due UCC suggestion. (1969, January 29). Corpus Christi Caller, p. 1.

[cxxxii] SACS admits 4 colleges. (1967, November 30). Dallas Morning News.

[cxxxiii] Jack Russell Blackmon. (2006, August 25). Obituaries. Corpus Christi Caller-Times. https://www.legacy.com/us/obituaries/ caller/name/jack-blackmon-obituary?pid=189526633

[cxxxiv] Deswysen, E. (1971, January 22). Blackmon selected chairman. Corpus Christi Caller, p. 1.

[cxxxv] Parmley, H. (1971, March 10). BGCT head opposes 'Church use of State'. Dallas Morning News.

[cxxxvi] Wrotenbery, C. R. (1998). Baptist Island College. Fort Worth, Texas: Eakin Press.

[cxxxvii] Wrotenbery, C. R. (1998). Baptist Island College. Fort Worth, Texas: Eakin Press.

[cxxxviii] Celelli, T. (2012). Missions through education: The continuing legacy of the University of Corpus Christi and the South Texas School of Christian Studies. In M. E. Williams, Texas Baptist History (pp. 69-80). Texas Baptist Historical Society.

[cxxxix] Hilton, T. (1977, July 2). Theology courses to be offered. Corpus Christi Caller, p. 20.

[cxl] Celelli, T. (2012). Missions through education: The continuing legacy of the University of Corpus Christi and the South Texas School of Christian Studies. In M. E. Williams, Texas Baptist History (pp. 69-80). Texas Baptist Historical Society.

[cxli] Hodnett, C. (2000, May 29). Baptist learning center quietly trains ministers - The center offers seminary certificates and master's degrees through other universities. Corpus Christi Caller-Times, B1.

[cxlii] Hodnett, C. (2000, May 29). Baptist learning center quietly trains ministers - The center offers seminary certificates and master's de grees through other universities. Corpus Christi Caller-Times, B1.

[cxliii] Celelli, T. (2012). Missions through education: The contin-uing legacy of the University of Corpus Christi and the South Texas School of Christian Studies. In M. E. Williams, Texas Baptist History (pp. 69-80). Texas Baptist Historical Society.

Transformation

Islanders Play Volleyball (Circa 1970)
*Special Collections and Archives, Mary and
Jeff Bell Library, Texas A&M
University-Corpus Christi*

Texas A&I University-Corpus Christi

On June 10, 1971 Texas Governor Preston Smith (1912-2003) signed a bill establishing Texas A&I University-Corpus Christi.[i] The signing took place in the newly restored library on Ward Island. This building had sustained considerable damage as many of the glass panels had been broken and over 10,000 volumes of the collection were exposed to water during Hurricane Celia.[ii] Less than a year later, the library and the university would be starting anew. The new A&I name and organizational control would become effective in the fall of 1973. In many ways, Hurricane Celia set in motion the events that led to the signing of this legislation to transform UCC into a sister university of Texas A&I University-Kingsville and Texas A&I University at Laredo which was being operated as a university center under A&I-Kingsville.

House Bill 275 and Senate Bill 131 were both filed during the 1971 legislative session to establish an upper-level university in Corpus Christi. Under the agreement, the BGCT would continue to provide funding for UCC during a transition period. Corpus Christi voters approved a $1.5 million bond package to pay off UCC's debt and purchase the campus from the BGCT.[iii] Additionally, private donations totaling $1.8 million were raised in support of a public institution.[iv] These efforts to ensure that the university was positioned to succeed would set the tone for a close relationship between the community and its new public university.

Texas A&I (Kingsville) had initially opposed any plan for a public institution of higher education in Corpus Christi, as A&I contended it would create competition. Kingsville argued they were capable of serving the area's needs and that the proximity of Corpus Christi to Kingsville (approximately 40 miles) meant that a state-supported university there would be a duplication of services and thus a waste of state resources. Texas A&I became supportive of, or at least stopped opposing, the plan after it was determined that the public university at Corpus Christi would join with A&I in a university system.[v]

Several important actions were taken in preparation for Texas A&I University-Corpus Christi. In April 1972, the Coordinating Board created an Office of the Chancellor to oversee the three A&I campuses. While the post was not immediately filled, the A&I Board of Regents, instructed the President of A&I-Kingsville, James C. Jernigan (1914-1996), to provide oversight to the incoming administration at A&I-Corpus Christi. He would be named Chancellor in 1973.[vi]

Dr. Jernigan earned his bachelor's and master's degrees from North Texas State College (University of North Texas), and a doctorate from the University of Chicago. Jernigan held several positions at Kingsville including Director of Student Personnel and Associate Professor of Education. He was appointed Dean in 1950 and President in 1962. The library at Texas A&M University-Kingsville was named after Jernigan in 1968, and he was named professor emeritus in 1987.

A Higher Education System

James C. Jernigan
Texas A&M University-Kingsville Archives

With the creation of the Office of the Chancellor, the three A&I universities were organized the University System of South Texas.[vii] This organization allowed for more coordination in areas such as degree offerings and budgeting. It was particularly important when seeking annual funding and approval for special items from the state legislature. Systems allow for efficiencies in many regards but add an additional organizational layer. They can also can create power struggles among institutions.

In the late 1960s and 1970s, "systemization" became common practice in Texas as the state's university systems expanded, particularly with
the University of Texas System and its largest campus in Austin. Arlington State College left its affiliation with Texas A&M University to
become part of the UT System in 1965 and was renamed The University of Texas at Arlington (UTA) in 1967. Also that year, a component
school of UT--Texas Western College of The University of Texas--was
renamed The University of Texas at El Paso. The University of Texas
System was further expanded with the founding of three new universities in 1969: UT Dallas, UT Permian Basin, and UT San Antonio. In
1979, Tyler State College joined the system as UT Tyler. In addition to
these universities, the UT System includes health science centers, medical schools, and UT Rio Grande Valley formed from the merger of UT
Pan American and UT Brownsville completed in 2015.[viii]

Changes in the organizational structure of the university systems in
Texas would have a bearing on the Island University on several occasions
through its history. Most importantly, expansion of the Texas A&M
University System would have a profound impact on the Texas A&I
universities. [ix]

The push for systemization would include other Texas institutions
as well with a strong bearing on how universities in the state are organized. With only two exceptions--Stephen F. Austin University, and
Texas Southern University--each of the other public universities in
Texas belongs to a system of higher education. Texas Tech University,
The University of North Texas, Texas State University, and the University of Houston all maintain systems with multiple institutions under
the governance of a board of regents and an executive officer titled as
chancellor. Organizational changes continue to the present.

In 2021, Texas Women's University transitioned from an independent university into a system with branches in Dallas and Houston organized as independent campuses.[x] Also in 2021, Midwestern State
University joined the Texas Tech University System.[xi]

Among the South Texas Universities

With the change to a public university and as a member of the A&I system, the Island University was under a much different governance structure than UCC. The system would now need to consider the academic offerings at the different campuses to determine how those programs fit with the boarder offerings at the sister institutions. Major initiatives and building projects would also be deliberated by the A&I Board of Regents. With the change to a public school, student tuition was lower as overall costs would now be supplemented though state appropriations. The core mission no longer included ministerial education but rather focused on the needs of underserved students primarily from South Texas. All of the A&I universities would serve large Hispanic populations. The focus on different student profiles was a distinctive change as the Island University would later have a plurality of Hispanic students and become a Hispanic-Serving Institution (HSI).

Texas A&I Kingsville had been founded in 1925 as South Texas Normal School, to provide qualified teachers in the region. Kingsville community leaders had lobbied for over two decades for passage of enabling legislation and funding for the college. Political reluctance, including two vetoes of enabling legislation, had delayed its founding. World War I further delayed initial funding even after the enabling legislation had been approved. The community was supportive of the college and several residents donated land for the campus.[xii]

Since its founding, Texas A&I Kingsville worked to serve the large Hispanic population of South Texas. Like UCC, the institution had changed names before the first student entered a classroom, taking the name of South Texas State Teachers College. The early names of the college emphasized the important mission of educating teachers, a particularly great need in South Texas. Initiatives at Kingsville included a program in ethnic studies and a long-standing program to promote bilingual education through teacher preparation. The prominence of nearby King Ranch enabled agricultural and wildlife programs to also become hallmark offerings.[xiii]

A New Focus

Daniel Whitney Halladay (1920-1980) was named president of A&I-CC. Halladay was previously the President at East Texas State University (ETSU) (later re-named Texas A&M University-Commerce) where he served from 1966-1972. Halladay, a native of California, held a B.A. from Pomona State (Cal Poly Pomona), an M.A. from Claremont University, and an Ed.D. from Columbia University in New York.[xiv] Halladay had built his career through stints at the University of Florida, Pomona College in California, University of Arkansas, and Columbia University.[xv] Halladay had resigned as ETSU president in 1972 upon the death of his ex-wife, Pat, by suicide.[xvi] The death took place at the President's Home on the campus following their recent divorce.[xvii]

Halladay had led East Texas State University during a time of rapid enrollment increases and oversaw a large construction program on campus. ETSU grew its enrollment from less than 7,000 to almost 9,000 during his six-year tenure. He would also grow the graduate offerings of ETSU.[xviii] Halladay oversaw similar enrollment increases and construction projects during his leadership of A&I-CC. In the first month of his tenure, Halladay stated, "We will build a university of stature and reputation that we think this community will be proud of." Halladay insisted that faculty be of high quality and adopted the slogan of "On to excellence" for a new development campaign.[xix]

Halladay faced an immediate need for funding to purchase the campus from the BGCT for the transition to occur. Surprisingly, Governor Smith vetoed a $1.5 million appropriation to purchase land, buildings, and equipment from the BGCT. Smith had understood that the state would not be liable for the cost of the campus.[xx] Halladay appealed to the Corpus Christi community to support their new public university by raising these critical funds.[xxi] In December 1972, a bond package was presented to Corpus Christi voters that included funds for the A&I-CC campus. Bonds were approved with 14,265 votes (78%) in favor to 3,979 votes against. This support allowed the change to state sponsorship occur without additional delay.[xxii][xxiii]

USST Chancellor Halladay, Vice-President of the USST Board of Directors Laurence A. McNeil, A&I-CC President Jernigan (1989)
Texas A&M University -Kingsville Archives

During the transition from UCC to A&I-CC, some A&I offices such as admissions, operated on the Ward Island campus alongside UCC. The President's office and other administrators held temporary offices in the United Saving Bank Building on Alameda Street. On campus, several dormitories were converted into office space.

UCC offered its last courses in the summer of 1973 with 12 faculty teaching approximately 30 courses including independent studies in an abridged summer term.[xxiv] The final UCC commencement ceremony had 32 graduates. A few UCC seniors would take religion courses temporarily offered by A&I-CC to finish their degrees.[xxv]

In September 1973, students of Texas A&I University-Corpus Christi would begin their classes on Ward Island. As an upper-level university, the new focus would be on providing transfer students with at least 60 credit hours to complete an undergraduate degree. In the first year as A&I-CC, a range of majors across four degrees--Bachelor of Business Administration, Bachelor of Arts, Bachelor of Science, and Bachelor of Music--were offered at the undergraduate level.[xxvi] A&I CC would initially offer four graduate programs, all through the College of Education.[xxvii] These offerings were a shift from UCC, which provided only undergraduate degrees, and would mark the beginning of many graduate offerings added over the coming decades.

Undergraduate students would now begin their studies elsewhere and transfer to the Island University having already completed their freshman and sophomore years. Many would study at Del Mar College, south of downtown Corpus Christi, to earn their lower-level credits before transferring as many students still do today. The new graduate offerings would allow individuals an opportunity to earn an advanced degree in Corpus Christi for the first time.[xxviii]

Texas A&I-Corpus Christi Mobile Marine Science Laboratory (n.d.)
Special Collections and Archives, Mary and Jeff Bell Library, Texas A&M University-Corpus Christi

These changes also meant that most students commuted to campus and were more likely to be older, working professionals.[xxix] The absence of a large residential population changed the feel of the campus and a different campus life emerged. Two dormitories did remain available on a first-come, first serve basis. Fraternities, sororities, and athletics programs were not a part of the campus life during this period.[xxx][xxxi]

Enrollment at A&I-CC would quickly increase even though the institution was no longer offering admission to freshman and sopho- mores. In the beginning of the 1974-1975 academic year, the Island University had an enrollment of 1,603 students, easily surpassing prior enrollment under UCC.[xxxii] This indicates that the demand for higher education was present, yet for a variety of reasons, UCC was not fully meeting demand.

Programs offered by A&I-CC spanned numerous disciplines across the four colleges: Arts and Humanities, Science and Technology, Edu- cation, and Business Administration. Night and weekend classes, as well as correspondence courses, were offered to appeal to working students. The organizational structure called for each of the four colleges to be led by a Dean. Within each college, departments were led by a faculty chair.[xxxiii]

Dr. Miriam Wagenschein Lectures in Class (n.d)
Special Collections and Archives, Mary and Jeff Bell Library, Texas A&M University -Corpus Christi

In 1973, Dr. Miriam Wagenschein (1922-2011)[xxxiv] was selected as dean of the new College of Arts and Humanities. The college would grow to have the largest number of faculty and degree program offerings. A Stanford University-educated sociologist, Dr. Wagenschein taught the first course in what would later be known as women's studies. Dean Wagenschein retired in 1998 after a 25 year career at the Island University. Two endowed professorships at TAMU-CC bear her name--one in sociology and the other in gender studies--furthering the important work she began.[xxxv]

Several building projects were undertaken during the A&I period that cumulatively would involve $20 million in facility construction over almost a decade.[xxxvi] This construction program would transform the campus and include many of the buildings that are still prominent features on the campus today. In 1975, a new 64,000-square-foot classroom building was constructed. This first building constructed after becoming a public institution was named Corpus Christi Hall in recognition of the support citizens had shown in funding the transition to a public institution and their ongoing contributions. President Halladay noted in the naming of the building, "The people of this city made our university possible." Other early projects included a new fieldhouse, handball courts, and remodeling of the administration building.[xxxvii] The change from a four-year university to an upper-level institution with graduate programs also altered the types of campus facilities needed. Less student housing was necessary, but the increased enrollment warranted additional classroom and office space. Miller Hall, a former dormitory for women, was remodeled for office and classroom space in 1975 with its name changing to Faculty Center II.[xxxviii] A new science building, fine arts building, and library were all constructed at A&I-CC. The science building was a 60,000-square-foot facility built at a cost of $2.5 million.

Corpus Christi Hall (Circa 1976)
Special Collections and Archives, Mary and Jeff Bell Library, Texas A&M University-Corpus Christi

The 93,800-square-foot Fine Arts Building cost $2.6 million and includes a 300-seat performance hall, theater, outdoor sculpture garden, photo lab, vocal and instrumental rooms, classrooms, offices, and a television studio. With the addition of this facility, art majors could be supported.[xxxix][xl] Within the building, the art gallery is named for Sylvan Weil (1888-1967), in recognition of a gift made by his wife, Ruth Weil, as a memorial to her husband. Mr. Weil was a Corpus Christi businessman and supporter of the arts.[xli]

Ruth and Sylvan Weil Gallery (2017)
Texas A&M University-Corpus Christi

Construction of the Science Building (circa 1977)
*Special Collections and Archives, Mary and Jeff Bell Library, Texas
A&M University-Corpus Christi*

With construction of a new library, the old library, known as the "round building," was repurposed to be used as an administration building. The new library would be 106,000 square feet and house up to 300,000 volumes.[xlii] The facility is named after Mary and Jeff Bell who gave a $1 million gift for the library. Jeff Bell (1921-2011) was a retired bank president from Portland, Texas.[xliii] The dedication of these three buildings on March 23, 1979 was presided over by Texas Governor Bill Clements who noted, "We must never forget our goal, our duty, and this is to give our citizens the basic building

Student Micah Knupp Performs as Mark Cohen in a Production of Rent (2016)
Texas A&M University-Corpus Christi

blocks needed to develop meaningful careers of their choice."[xliv]

Halladay would be named Chancellor of the three A&I campuses in 1976 and remain in the position as the system itself was renamed to University System of South Texas. On July 12, 1980, Halladay unexpectedly passed away in his sleep while visiting family in Mississippi. Halladay was 59 at the time of his death, and news of his loss was a shock to the community.[xlv] Halladay proved an able administrator and worked to grow higher education in Texas at two universities and as the head of a university system.

Except for the short-lived name of Arts and Technology College, the Island University would bear the Texas A&I University-Corpus Christi name for the fewest number of years among its several names. Under Halladay and his successor, Barney Alan Sugg, the transformation from a private to public institution, the shift in mission, and a sharpened focus on upper-level coursework greatly changed the nature of the university. This change also set in motion the growth and expansion that defined the decades to follow. Many new traditions would form in the next decades and build an identity that is much different than that of UCC. The name change also ushered in a tradition of referring to the institution as the "Island University" in marketing literature and by students and faculty.[xlvi] The distinctive nature of an island-based campus would remain a positive attribute for students in selecting a location for their studies.

Corpus Christi State University Entrance Sign (Circa 1978)
Mary and Jeff Bell Library, Special Collections and Archives Department, Texas A&M University-Corpus Christi

Corpus Christi State University

Another name change marked the beginning of the 1977-1978 academic year as Corpus Christi State University (CCSU) became part of the newly founded University System of South Texas (USST). Governor Dolph Briscoe (1923-2010)[xlvii] signed the bill authorizing the change on May 27, 1977.[xlviii]

On August 22, 1978, CCSU student Barbara Smith broke a bottle of champagne on the school's entrance sign located on Ocean Drive to mark the official change.[xlix] President Sugg put up the first letter of the new name on the entrance sign. Each of the college deans then followed by adding letters.[l]

Corpus Christi State University Administrators Affix Letters to the Entrance Sign for the Newly Re-named University (1977)

Mary and Jeff Bell Library, Special Collections and Archives Department, Texas A&M University-Corpus Christi

CCSU was not the only name under consideration. Students and board members alike took positions on what the new name should be. The board of directors of Texas A&I-Corpus Christi had narrowly approved, in a 4-3 vote, to recommend to the Texas Legislature that the name of University of Corpus Christi be used.[li] Had the UCC name been approved, the university would have reverted to the same name that was in use while it was a private school. Concerns were expressed over the UCC name as it had ultimately not been successful. Others desired to keep the A&I name intact as the Kingsville campus had national recognition due to their successful football program. University of the Gulf Coast was also proposed.[lii] Legislators, spearheaded by Texas State Senator Carlos F. Truan, Sr. (1935-2012), drafted the bill to bestow the name Corpus Christi State University.[liii]

Seal of Corpus Christi State University (Circa 1978)

Mary and Jeff Bell Library, Special Collections and Archives Department, Texas A&M University-Corpus Christi

A longtime advocate of the university, Sen. Truan served for 33 years in the Texas Legislature, first in the House of Representatives from 1969-1976 representing Nueces (Corpus Christi) and Kleberg (Kingsville) Counties. He was then elected to the Texas Senate in 1977 and would retire from the upper chamber in 2003 having been its Dean, or longest serving member. Truan was a force to be reckoned with in the Senate. He once filibustered a bill for 20 hours and would often wear his white tennis shoes to the Senate floor as a threat to filibuster a measure on which he disagreed.[liv] The Senate district Truan represented included Brooks, Jim Wells, Kenedy, Kleberg, Nueces, San Patricio, Willacy, and part of Hidalgo counties. As such, he represented both CCSU and A&I-Kingsville. He was an important figure in the organization of these universities and worked to shepherd legislation on their behalf through the legislature.

Truan was born in Kingsville and graduated from Texas A&I (Kingsville) in 1959. He and his family resided in Corpus Christi where he owned an insurance business.[lv] Truan passed away in 2012 at the age of 76.[lvi] The Carlos F. Truan Natural Resources Building at Texas A&M University-Corpus Christi is named after the Senator. The 100,000-square-foot facility opened in 1993 and is located west of Island Drive. It was attained through a $10 million legislative appropriation spearheaded by

Texas State Senator Carlos F. Truan, Sr.
Texas A&M University-Kingsville Archives

Truan. Under a unique arrangement, the building houses several state agency offices focused on natural resources in addition to university offices.[lvii] A unique entity housed in the facility is the National Spill Control School. The school began by offering courses on oil spill control in 1977 and has steadily added training courses over its history. The school was included in the Oil Pollution Control Act of 1990 and has been recognized as a leading entity in this field.[lviii]

Adjacent to the NRC is the Conrad Blucher Institute for Surveying & Science. This institute is named for Conrad M. Blucher (1885-1977), an important figure in the development of Nueces County. Conrad's grandparents, Anton Felix Hans Hellmuth von Blucher and his wife Maria, came to Texas in 1849 from their native Germany. Von Blucher was educated at the University of Berlin in civil engineering, law, and languages. The Bluchers settled in Nueces County on a plot of land that for a time was known as Blucherville due to the large number of their family's homes occupying the area. Blucherville once had a prized view of Corpus Christi Bay from a highpoint in the bluffs west of the downtown area. The view of the bay is now obstructed from Blucherville by downtown office towers. Blucher Park in Corpus Christi occupies part of this area, while three of the impressive family homes in the adjacent neighborhood are used as professional offices. These homes are among the oldest residential structures in their original location within the city.[lix]

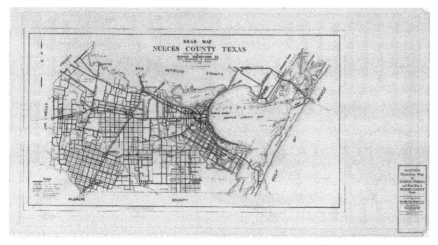

Nueces County Map, Blucher Engineering Co. (1950)
Charles H. F. von Blucher Family Papers, Collection 4, Mary and Jeff Bell Library, Special Collections and Archives Department, Texas A&M University-Corpus Christi

The family's gift to the university would reflect their profession. Three generations of Bluchers would serve as Nueces County surveyor, totaling over 100 years of service. After beginning in 1849, Felix von Blucher would be succeeded by his son, Charles, in 1882. Conrad would succeed his father in the post in 1934, retiring in 1954. In 1975, Conrad and his wife, Zula, dedicated their estate to CCSU to foster the study of surveying. Upon the death of Mrs. Blucher in 1986, the $2 million gift funded the institute which bears his name. The Conrad Blucher Institute was dedicated on May 17, 1987 and soon offered courses in surveying.[lx]

The Blucher Institute would transition from traditional surveying technics to Geographic Information Systems (GIS) as the technology rapidly advanced. Degree programs at the undergraduate, master's, and doctoral level are now offered in the field of GIS. Further, through its several laboratories, the institute works with other entities on campus to conduct research. Notably, the Coastal Dynamics Lab conducts monitoring of the Gulf of Mexico.[lxi]

A small yet profound monument on Ward Island pays tribute to this program as well as one of its long-time directors. Upon the retirement of Dr. Gary Jeffress in 2018, a permanent GIS position "Jeffress 2018" was published in the National Geodetic Survey database. This point serves as a geodetic control point in the National Spatial Reference System (NSRS).[lxii]

Leadership

CCSU President Halladay was named the chancellor of the newly formed USST and located the headquarters for the system in Corpus Christi. Halladay's tenure as chancellor would be short lived, as he unexpectedly passed away in 1980.[lxiii] [lxiv]

Dr. D. Whitney Halladay (Circa 1980)

Alumni Update, December 1980. Special Collections and Archives, Mary and Jeff Bell Library, Texas A&M University-Corpus Christi

Dr. Duane M. Leach (1935-) would be named the next chancellor of the University System of South Texas. Leach had become president of A&I Kingsville in 1977 and would move the USST headquarters to a property adjacent to the King Ranch, three miles from the Kingsville campus.[lxv] The system offices would be in the former home of Robert R. (Bobby) Shelton (1935-1994), a descendant of Richard King, founder of the King Ranch. Under the arrangement, five rooms totaling 5,000-square-feet of the home were remodeled to serve as administrative offices.[lxvi]

Dr. Duane Leach
(Circa 1980)
*Alumni Update,
December 1980.
Special Collections
and Archives, Mary
and Jeff Bell Library,
Texas A&M
University-Corpus
Christi*

Richard King (1824-1885) and his wife Henrietta Chamberlain (1832-1925) built one of the largest ranches in Texas. King, a native of New York, had little formal education as he worked on riverboats from a young age after breaking an apprenticeship and fleeing westward. King became a riverboat pilot at age sixteen and later a partner in two riverboat companies that operated on the Rio Grande River.

A speculator by nature, King bought significant portions of undeveloped land in South Texas. His business interests were wide yet integrated in a manner that allowed for maximization of profits such as through his development of the means to transport ranch products to large markets. King would be a strong advocate for South Texas to have access to ports.[lxvii][lxviii]

Henrietta would be instrumental in building the ranch for the decade following the passing of her husband. She would transfer the responsibilities of running the ranch to her son-in-law, Robert J. Kleberg, Sr. (1853-1932) in 1895. King Ranch remains a working ranch with over 825,000 acres and business interests spanning cattle ranching, natural resources, farming, recreational hunting, and luxury goods. The brand of the King Ranch, the "Running W", is a widely recognized symbol. Products spanning from pickup trucks to restaurants carry the brand as a badge of quality. The King and Kleberg families have donated to numerous causes in South Texas including for the establishment of what would become Texas A&M University-Kingsville. The City of Kingsville was established in 1904 on property granted by Kleberg and is named in honor of Richard King.[lxix]

"A Thoroughbred" King's Ranch, Texas. (1908)
Library of Congress, STEREO U.S. GEOG FILE - Texas--Kingsville

While office space was generously provided by the King family, the arrangement moved the USST offices from Corpus Christi to a location that was closer, both physically and symbolically, to Kingsville. Leach's immediate past position as the A&I (Kingsville) president likely entered into the equation. His sentiment towards Kingsville suggested an unequal positioning of universities within the USST. In 1977, while serving as A&I-Kingsville's President, Leach defended the new organization as a system noting, "Texas A&I as the exceptional flagship of the system and expect it to remain so in the future."[lxx] The struggle over position within the system would often be framed in relative terms. A common argument in favor of the arrangement was that the system provided more strength in sum than the constituent campuses would on their own. However, the sentiment that one USST university was more equal than others would be present periodically as the system members found themselves linked by a common organizational structure, culture, and geography.

Leach would resign to become the president of the University of Texas-Permian Basin in Odessa in the fall of 1983.[lxxi] Before leaving, Leach commissioned a report on the higher education needs of South Texas. Among other findings, the report noted that citizens of the region felt there was a lack of graduate and professional programs. At the time, the region did not have a medical, veterinarian, law, or pharmacy school. Leach reflected that he felt that the banning together of the three A&I universities into USST had benefited each school by collectively raising their profiles. He further noted that CCSU was mainly serving the needs of its immediate geographic area and that the more professional centered programs, such as computer science and business administration, were in high demand.[lxxii]

The need for additional professional and graduate education was noted in 1987 during committee hearings of the Texas Legislature. When compared to North Texas, in particular, the USST and other South Texas universities offered few doctoral and graduate level educational options.[lxxiii]

In 1983, Dr. Lawrence K. Pettit (1937-) was named the next Chancellor of the University System of South Texas. Pettit, a native of Montana, earned degrees at the University of Montana (B.A.), Washington University in St. Louis (M.A.), and the University of Wisconsin, Madison (Ph.D. in Political Science). He worked in higher education with faculty stints at Pennsylvania State University and Montana State University.

Pettit had also pursued a career in politics. After working for members of Congress in Washington, he led the campaign to elect Thomas L. Judge (1934-2006) as governor of Montana. Following the campaign, he worked on the governor's staff. Governor Judge would name Pettit as the first Higher Education Commissioner for Montana upon creation of the position by a new state constitution adopted in 1972. Pettit held this position for six years and oversaw the Montana University System which consisted of six campuses. He unsuccessfully ran for U.S. Representative from Montana in 1980.

Left to Right: Mary Lewis Kleberg; Larry Pettit; Libby Pettit; Mrs. Franklin; A&I
Kingsville University President Dr. Billy "Bill" Franklin
Texas A&M University-Kingsville Archives, A2017-074.0060

At the time of his appointment to lead USST, Pettit was serving as
Associate Commissioner of the Coordinating Board of the Texas College and University System.[lxxiv] Pettit took the job at the Coordinating Board with the understanding that he would like to return to lead a
university or university system. The USST chancellor position provided
this opportunity. Upon his departure from USST he would serve as the
head of Southern Illinois University from 1986 to 1991, and then as
President of Indiana University of Pennsylvania, ultimately retiring in
2003. Pettit remains an advocate for higher education during his retirement in Montana.[lxxv][lxxvi][lxxvii]

Pettit was ambitious and desired USST to increase its national and
international presence. He considered the job to be less stressful than
his prior positions and used his energies to engage in speaking and writing engagements that elevated the system in notable circles. Pettit also
secured agreements with Honduras, El Salvador, and Guatemala to allow their students to study at USST universities.

Pettit would make headlines by stating that South Texas was not receiving similar resources in the way of professional and graduate education when compared to other areas of the state. He worked towards treating Hispanic universities in a similar manner to majority Black institutions (Historically Black Universities or HBU's) for purposes of increased support to offset systemic disparities. This was an important consideration and part of a larger push for increased resources to be devoted to USST schools. In response to a larger movement, additional doctoral programs were started in South Texas at the USST institutions and Pan American University.

This movement included a lawsuit filed by The League of United Latin American Citizens (LULAC). *LULAC v. Richards et al.* was a class-action lawsuit filed in 1987 that charged the state with discrimination against Mexican Americans in South Texas due to inadequate funding of higher education in the region. In response, the Texas Legislature passed the South Texas/Border Initiative in 1989 to improve institutions across South Texas including CCSU. The changes seen in the system re-organization across Texas higher education were at least partly in response to this lawsuit and the overarching concern over equity. The South Texas/Border institutions received over $880 million in special item funding from 1990 through 2003.[lxxviii][lxxix]

A 2003 report by the Texas Higher Education Coordinating Board to the Texas House of Representatives Border and International Affairs Committee again noted the lack of a law, medical, dental, or professional school in the region.[lxxx] A pharmacy school named for former State Representative Irma Rangel (1931-2003) from Kingsville would open there in 2006. However, the pharmacy school is part of the Texas A&M University Health Science Center, not TAMU-Kingsville. The College offers a Doctor of Pharmacy (PharmD) in a four-year degree track. There is a partnership to allow pharmacy students to simultaneously earn a Master of Business Administration Degree from TAMU Kingsville. Further, the creation of UT-Rio Grande Valley would bring a medical school to the region in 2013.

Dr. B. Alan Sugg (n.d.)
Special Collections and Archives, Mary and Jeff Bell Library, Texas A&M University-Corpus Christi

During this period, CCSU would also have a new president in Barney Alan Sugg (1938-). He was serving as Vice President for Academic Affairs at Corpus Christi in 1972 having held a similar position at East Texas State University. Sugg joined Halladay in Corpus Christi after working under him in student affairs at Arkansas and then East Texas State University. Sugg would become A&I-CC President upon Halladay's promotion to Chancellor of the USST.[lxxxi]

The Sugg family enjoyed South Texas especially seafood and trips to beaches. Sugg took Spanish classes from Del Mar College to "better pronounce Hispanic names." In 2008, President Sugg recalled that his daughters both grew up in Corpus Christi. For a time, the daughters raised horses and Sugg pulled a horse trailer with the family station wagon. In an in-depth interview, thirty-six years after leaving Corpus Christi, he noted the community support and pride for their new university. [lxxxii]

Sugg would serve as CCSU president for 13 years and for a period as interim USST Chancellor upon the departure of Pettit. He indicated at the time of the interim appointment that he was not interested in the Chancellor position and desired to remain CCSU president. However, he left CCSU to head the University of Arkansas System in 1990. A native of Arkansas, he enjoyed a long and favorable career growing that system from 30,000 to 70,000 students by his retirement in 2011.[lxxxiii]

In 1986, 3,855 students were enrolled at CCSU while Kingsville was the larger campus with 5,057 students during that same year.[lxxxiv] The CCSU campus was rapidly changing and modernizing. By 1978, only two of the original naval buildings remained and those were slated for removal to make way for additional parking lots and buildings. The Arts Department occupied one of the last two buildings while the other was the home of long-time maintenance worker Jake Saldana.[lxxxv]

Programs at CCSU continued a steady expansion. In the late 1970s, the process for adding graduate programs in psychology, public administration, nursing, and computer science was initiated. Funding for these programs was not immediately approved, but they would all eventually become popular degree offerings.[lxxxvi] For undergraduates, a program in medical records was also planned.[lxxxvii]

Teacher education had been an important and successful program offering at UCC with an onsite kindergarten and first grade to assist with the training of teachers. CCSU expanded these programs for educating teachers by utilizing

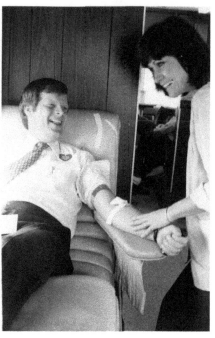

Dr. B. Alan Sugg (n.d.)
Special Collections and Archives, Mary and Jeff Bell Library, Texas A&M University-Corpus Christi

classroom experiences. The Teacher Training Institute became recognized across the state for quality teacher training.[lxxxviii][lxxxix] In a similar fashion, CCSU added a Teaching and Learning Center for Young Children in 1978. Operated through the College of Education, this program began the long-standing presence of elementary age children attending school on Ward Island. Today, the Early Childhood Development Center continues to serve in this capacity.[xc] The facility was named after Blanche Davis Moore in 1996. Blanche Moore Elementary School, another Corpus Christi Independent School District cam pus in the southern part of the city, is also named after Mrs. Moore in recognition of a real estate gift to build a school.

Blanche Davis Moore (1904-1983) was a philanthropist whose estate funded The Allen Lovelace Moore and Blanche Davis Moore Foundation in 1993 primarily for the benefit of Nueces County children. Initial funding of the foundation came from the sale of 160 acres of the Moore's farmland adjacent to South Padre Island Drive (SPID) much of which is now occupied by Moore Plaza Shopping Center.[xci] The Moore's paid about $200 an acre for the property in 1944 from earnings off their North Beach arcade and concessions businesses. At the time of the purchase, the property was farmland located off Lexington Boulevard (later re-named SPID). Mr. Moore, who went by the nick name "Dinty", rightly predicted that the property would one day be the center of Corpus Christi.

Main Street of North Beach Tourist District, Corpus Christi, Texas (1939)
Lee, Russell, Library of Congress. LC-USF34- 032251-D [P&P] LOT 596

The student profile during the CCSU years was older and more professionally focused than during the UCC years. The nature of the upper-level campus required students to have completed coursework previously.[xcii] Thus, the average age was higher when compared with four-year institutions.

With an average age of 30, CCSU had a student population that was well above the state-wide mean. Most students worked full-time, and many were enrolled in CCSU graduate programs. In the fall 1980 commencement, 217 degrees were awarded with 60 (27%) of these being master's degrees.[xciii]

Students Celebrate the Completion of Their Master's Degree (2018)
Texas A&M University-Corpus Christi

Many CCSU students came from the surrounding area, as was the case for Ricardo L. Rodriguez. A navy veteran of the Vietnam War, Rodriguez attended CCSU after obtaining an associate's degree from Del Mar College. He worked while attending school and was a first-generation college graduate. His accounting degree would prove an asset as he was elected Mayor of Robstown in 1980. Rodriguez would spend his career in public service and be selected as Chief Financial Officer for the Corpus Christi Independent School District. While Rodriguez was a stand-out alumnus, his story resonates with other graduates as many first-generation, veteran, employed, and older students would attend the Island University.[xciv]

Hon. Ricardo L. Rodriguez, Mayor of Robstown, Texas (1980)
Alumni Update, June 1980. Special Collections and Archives, Mary and Jeff Bell Library, Texas A&M University-Corpus Christi

As the university changed its offerings, and upon expansion to again serve freshman and sophomores, the average age of students would decline, again shifting the profile of the student body. More students would choose to live on campus. Seabreeze Hall was opened in 1983 to house 80 students as Warren Hall held 84 students.[xcv] Two more residence halls were opened in the fall of 1984.[xcvi]

Re-organizations, Systemization, and Mergers, Oh My!

With the large expansion of the University of Texas System in 1969, administrators in Kingsville began to worry about the expansion of UT into South Texas. UT had considerable resources and name recognition. Any expansion or acquisition of an existing university by the UT System could lead to stiff competition for recruitment of students across the southern region of the state. One means of defense was to strengthen the existing USST system by attracting additional universities to join.

Pan American College in Edinburg, a border city in far South Texas, was unsuccessfully solicited to join USST as legislation was filed that would fold Pan American into the USST in 1987.[xcvii] While this effort failed, the attempt illustrated the push for systemization of the South Texas universities. Pan American would join the UT System as UT Pan American in 1989.[xcviii]

Different proposals materialized involving the organization of the Island University, other institutions in the region, and the university systems. In the mid-1980s, discussions over the organization of the South Texas Universities occurred. Larry E. Temple (1935-), Chairman of the Select Committee on Higher Education, issued a report recommending a merger of the Kingsville and Corpus Christi campuses into one university. The report went on to recommend that the headquarters of this new university be in Corpus Christi since it was the larger of the two cities and being an urban area likely allowed for more enrollment growth.[xcix]

Joining a larger university system was also a means to advocate for more equity for students and institutions in South Texas. A 1988 report indicated that the state spent $43 per student in South Texas versus $103 per student in the rest of the state. There were significant inequities present in facilities and academic programs because of this disparity.[c]

During this time, a plan for CCSU to become a comprehensive school was under discussion. Sugg was an advocate of expanding offerings to again include freshman and sophomores. However, this idea was met with resistance from A&I-Kingsville and Del Mar College. The enrollment at Kingsville peaked in 1975 at 7,641 but by the end of the decade dropped to 6,140. CCSU increased from 1,603 students in 1975 to 2,748 in 1979. This figure was well below some growth projections, notably the projection of 5,000 students by 1980 as made by Halladay in 1972 at the time of A&I-CC's beginning.[ci] Kingsville officials expressed concern that increases at CCSU had come at their expense. Adding offerings at the lower level would potentially exacerbate Kingsville's enrollment decline.[cii] Similarly, Del Mar College's reluctance is not surprising as many local students attended the college as their preferred conduit for earning the 60 credit hours necessary to enroll at CCSU. Should CCSU offer lower level courses, many of these same students may choose to begin their studies at CCSU as opposed to transferring at the roughly halfway mark in their undergraduate studies. In 1987, public hearings on the expansion of CCSU were held in Corpus Christi as the Texas Legislature was considering legislation on the matter.[ciii]

Proposals were offered for Del Mar and CCSU to be merged. Del Mar had opened in 1935 under control of the Corpus Christi Independent School District. The community college was incorporated as an in dependent college district in 1951. The incompatibility of the mission of the two institutions-Del Mar had robust vocational offerings and associate degrees-did not work well together. Del Mar received local tax revenue; a source of income not available to upper-level institutions such as CCSU. Alternatively, CCSU received more state funding and assistance with other large capital outlays. The mixing of these sources of income had not been implemented previously and posed considerable obstacles, legal and otherwise. Significant changes to state law would be necessary to address funding issues and governance.[civ] State budget woes were the catalyst for much of these discussions as it proved difficult to grant CCSU four-year status and fund the expansion.[cv]

Similar discussions took place during this period such as on merging Laredo State University and Laredo Junior College. Other states, such as Florida and Illinois, had attempted this model and did not find this method of organization to be particularly beneficial.[cvi]

During the 1987 Legislative session, a bill granting four-year status to CCSU as well as the addition of University of Pan America to the USST system did not pass. This bill again illustrated the push for South Texas universities to band together under the umbrella of a system.[cvii] Plans to address the underlying desire for a four-year institution and a continued push for systemization would be acted on in 1989 with implications for all the South Texas universities and significant expansion of the Texas A&M University System.

President B. Alan Sugg, Dr. Hector P. Garcia and Dr. Fred Cervantes at Corpus Christi State University Commencement Exercises

Dr. Hector P. García Papers, Collection 5, Box 433, Folder 2. Special Collections and Archives, Mary and Jeff Bell Library, Texas A&M University -Corpus Christi

References

[i] Hunter, A., & Hunter, L. G. (2000). Texas A&M University Kingsville. Charleston, SC: Arcadia.

[ii] Wrotenbery, R. (1998). Baptist Island College. Fort Worth, Texas: Eakin Press.

[iii] Hunter, C. A., & Hunter, L. G. (2000). Texas A&M University Kingsville. Charleston, SC: Arcadia.

[iv] A&I-CC classroom building named 'Corpus Christi Hall'. (1975, April 18). Corpus Christi Caller, 12.

[v] Hunter, A., & Hunter, L. G. (2000). Texas A&M University Kingsville. Charleston, SC: Arcadia.

[vi] Hunter, C. A., & Hunter, L. G. (2000). Texas A&M University Kingsville. Charleston, SC: Arcadia.

[vii] Hunter, C. A., & Hunter, L. G. (2000). Texas A&M University Kingsville. Charleston, SC: Arcadia.

[viii] History of the UT (2020, August 23). The University of Texas System. https://www.utsystem.edu/offices/chancellor/history-ut-system

[ix] Cardozier, R. (n.d.). Higher Education. Texas State Historical Association. https://www.tshaonline.org/handbook/entries/ higher-education

[x] Texas Woman's University. (2021). Bill establishing TWU System becomes law. https://twu.edu/news-events/news/bill-establishing twu-system-becomes-law/

[xi] Texas Tech (2021, June 8). Texas Tech University System welcomes Midwestern State University.https://www.texas tech.edu/stories/21-06-ttu-system-welcomes-msu-texas.php

[xii] Hunter, C. A., & Hunter, L. G. (2000). Texas A&M University Kingsville. Charleston, SC: Arcadia.

[xiii] Hunter, C. A., & Hunter, L. G. (2000). Texas A&M University Kingsville. Charleston, SC: Arcadia.

[xiv] Chancellor Halladay dies suddenly. (1980, July 13). Corpus Christi Caller-Times, p. 1.

[xv] Promising choice. (1972, May 10). Corpus Christi Caller, p. 14.

[xvi] Whitney Halladay. (2020, August 29). Northeast Texas Digital Collection. https://dmc.tamuc.edu/ digital/collection/historic et/id/ 2825/

[xvii] Fumes kill ex-wife of university head (1972, February 25). Corpus Christi Caller, p. 19.

[xviii] ETSU head takes A&I post at (1972, May 6). Dallas Morning News.

[xix] Jackson, M. (1972, May 16). The aim is a university of excellence and stature. Corpus Christi Caller, p. 14.

[xx] Reiste, B. (1983, April 10). Public determination made CCSU Corpus Christi Caller-Times, p. 1.

[xxi] Phelps, (1972, July 28). Support for A&I-CC urged. Corpus Christi Caller, p. 14.

[xxii] Gonzalez, (1972, November 28). A&I-CC bond issue pushed by Halladay. Corpus Christi Caller, p. 20.

[xxiii] A&I-CC fund proposal less than (1972, December 14). Corpus Christi Caller, p. 35.

[xxiv] Davis, A. (1973, May 6). UCC summer school still open this year. Corpus Christi Caller, p. 11.

[xxv] Reiste, B. (1983, April 10). Public determination made CCSU succeed. Corpus Christi Caller-Times, p. 1.

[xxvi] Four bachelor degrees planned. (1973, July 1). Corpus Christi Caller.

[xxvii] Rodman, (1973, May 6). Time has come for Texas A&I CC to operate. Corpus Christi Caller, p. 11.

[xxviii] Hunter, C. A., & Hunter, L. G. (2000). Texas A&M University Kingsville. Charleston, SC: Arcadia.

[xxix] Kreneck, H., Gammage, B., & Paschal, S. (2007). Texas A&M University-Corpus Christi: The Island University: 60 years, 1947-2007.

Texas A&M University-Corpus Christi: Division of Institutional Advancement.

[xxx] Reiste, B. (1983, April 10). Public determination made CCSU succeed. Corpus Christi Caller-Times, p. 1.

[xxxi] Rodman, (1973, May 6). Time has come for Texas A&I CC to operate. Corpus Christi Caller, p. 11.

[xxxii] Young, B. (2020, August 26). Texas A&M University Corpus Christi. Texas State Historical Association Handbook of Texas: https://www.tshaonline.org/handbook/entries/texas-a-m-university corpus-christi

[xxxiii] Halladay, W. (1972, December 31). Texas A&I-CC plans to be flexible, original in scope. Corpus Christi Caller-Times, p. 81.

[xxxiv] Miriam Wagenschein. (2011, July 31). Obituaries. Corpus Christi Caller-Times. https://www.legacy.com/us/obituaries/caller/ name/miriam-wagenschein-obituary?n=miriam-wagen schein&pid= 189544437

[xxxv] Howard, H. (1998, May 4). A&M-Corpus Christi dean retiring after 25 years Miriam Wagenschein, first teacher of women's studies, to be honored at reception Corpus Christi Caller-Times, B2.

[xxxvi] Branning, C. (1980, November 12). Committee launches search for new A&I Corpus Christi Caller, p. 17.

[xxxvii] A&I-CC classroom building named 'Corpus Christi Hall'. (1975, April 18). Corpus Christi Caller, 12.

[xxxviii] A&I-CC faculty office space ready. (1975, January 8). Corpus Christi Caller, 10.

[xxxix] Construction booming at A&I-CC. (1977, March 3). Corpus Christi Caller, 23.

[xl] Branning, C. (1979, July 13). Welfare group's stay at A&I is explained. Corpus Christi Caller, p. 15.

[xli] A&I building will include Weil gallery. (1976, October 28). Corpus Christi Caller, 23.

[xlii] Construction booming at A&I-CC. (1977, March 3). Corpus Christi Caller, 23.

[xliii] Barbee, D. (2000, September 21). A&M-CC due big donation. Corpus Christi Caller-Times, p. 1.

[xliv] Callaway, M. (1979, April 11). Clements calls for quality education at CCSU dedication. Corpus Christi Caller, p. 15.

[xlv] Chancellor Halladay dies suddenly. (1980, July 13). Corpus Christi Caller-Times, 1.

[xlvi] Kreneck, T. H., Gammage, B., & Paschal, S. (2007). Texas A&M University-Corpus Christi: The Island University: 60 years, 1947-2007. Texas A&M University-Corpus Christi: Division of Institutional Advancement.

[xlvii] Hevesi, D. (2010, June 28). Dolph Briscoe, Texas Governor in the '70s, Dies at 87. The New York Times. https://www.nytimes.com/2010/06/29/us/29briscoe.html.

[xlviii] Briscoe to sign CCSU bill today. (1977, May 27). Corpus Christi Caller, p. 17.

[xlix] Name makes a splash. (1977, August 23). Corpus Christi Caller, p. 20.

[l] A&I-CC changes name Monday. (1977, August 20). Corpus Christi Caller, p. 16.

[li] New name bill. (1977, February 4). Corpus Christi Caller, p. 13.

[lii] Ozio, R. (1977, January 13). A&I students like new name. Corpus Christi Caller.

[liii] New name bill. (1977, February 4). Corpus Christi Caller, p. 13.

[liv] Spruill, R. (2012, April 18). Truan at rest in Austin grave. Corpus Christi Caller-Times, p. 1.

[lv] Fernandez, S. L. (2001, December 19). Sen. Truan bows out of race for office - He cites demands of campaign, wants time with family. Corpus Christi Caller-Times, p. 1.

[lvi] Spruill, R. (2012, April 18). Truan at rest in Austin grave. Corpus Christi Caller-Times, p. 1.

[lvii] Parker, D. (1996, August 7). $10 million A&M-CC center is dedicated. Corpus Christi Caller-Times.

[lviii] History. (2021). The National Spill Control School. Texas A&M University-Corpus Christi. https://nscs.tamucc.edu/history.html

[lix] Shattuck, H. (2000, October 1). Corpus Christi: Blucher House stands tall in town's history. Houston Chronicle. https://www.chron.com/life/travel/article/Corpus-Christi-Blucher House-stands-tall-in-2015772.php

[lx] Phelps, G. (1987, August 13). Fund could lead to survey degree program. Corpus Christi Caller-Times, p. 48.

[lxi] History. (2020, August 29). Conrad Blucher Institute. Texas A&M University-Corpus Christi. https://www.conradblucherinstitute.org/history

[lxii] Commemorating Dr. Jeffress. (2018). Conrad Blucher Institute. Texas A&M University-Corpus Christi. https://cbi.tamucc.edu/Commemorating-Dr-Gary-]effress/

[lxiii] Hunter, C. A., & Hunter, L. G. (2000). Texas A&M University Kingsville. Charleston, SC: Arcadia.

[lxiv] Goodwin, B. (1983, July 5). Leach cites need for long-range plan. Corpus Christi Caller, p. 14.

[lxv] Hunter, C. A., & Hunter, L. G. (2000). Texas A&M University Kingsville. Charleston, SC: Arcadia.

[lxvi] Branning, C. (1981, April 26). New offices are fit kings. Corpus Christi Caller-Times, p. 79.

[lxvii] About Us. (2021). King Ranch. https://king-ranch.com/

[!xviii] Ashton, J. & Sneed, E. P. (n.d.). Handbook of Texas Online. Texas State Historical Association. https://www.tshaonline.org/handbook/entries/king-ranch

[lxix] Ashton, J. & Sneed, E. P. (n.d.). Handbook of Texas Online. Texas State Historical Association. https://www.tshaonline.org/handbook/entries/king-ranch

[lxx] Newton, B. (1977, October 14). Leach urges cooperation among universities. Corpus Christi Caller, p. 13.

[lxxi] Goodwin, B. (1983, August 2). Dr. Pettit is named chancellor of South Texas university group. Corpus Christi Caller, p. 1.

[lxxii] Goodwin, B. (1983, July 5). Leach cites need for long-range plan. Corpus Christi Caller, p. 14.

[lxxiii] Davis, J. (1987, March 17). S. Texas system is praised. Corpus Christi Caller, p. 14.

[lxxiv] Goodwin, B. (1983, August 2). Dr. Pettit is named chancellor of South Texas university group. Corpus Christi Caller, p. 1.

[lxxv] Pettit, L. K. (2021, February 26). Montana must keep partisan politics out of education. https://helenair.com/opinion/columnists/montana-must-keeppartisan-politics-out-of-education/article9dd9a054-l79a-5Sa4-94e3-28c788704fce.html

[lxxvi] Bio. (2021). Lawrence K. Pettit. http://www.lawrencekpettit.com/bio

[lxxvii] Goodwin, B. (1983, August 2). Dr. Pettit is named chancellor of South Texas university group. Corpus Christi Caller, p. 1.

[lxxviii] Acosta, T. P. (n.d.). Mexican American Legal Defense and Educational Fund. Texas State Historical Association. https://www.tshaonline.org/handbook/ entries/mexican-american-legal-defense-and-educational-fund

[lxxix] Carales, V. D. & Doran, E. (2020). The pursuit of equal educational opportunity: A historical analysis of the South Texas/Border Initiative. Educational Policy. https://lib.dr.iastate.edu/cgi/viewcontent.cgi?article=1167&con text=edu_pubs

[lxxx] Flack, T. (2003). Presentation on South Texas Border Initiatives. House Border and International Affairs Committee. Texas House of Representatives. 0592.PDF http://www.thecb.state.tx.us/DocID/PDF/

[lxxxi] Sugg, B. A. (2008, February 13). Scott Lunsford interviewed Alan Sugg. (S. Lunsford, Interviewer). file:///D:/Download/ TRANSSUGG-B-Alan-Memories-20080213-FINAL.pdf

[lxxxii] Sugg, B. A. (2008, February 13). Scott Lunsford interviewed Alan Sugg. (S. Lunsford, Interviewer). file:///D:/Download/TRANS-SUGG-B-Alan-Memories-20080213-FINAL.pdf

[lxxxiii] Past Presidents. (2020, August 29). Retrieved from University of Arkansas System. https://www.uasys.edu/leadership/office-of the-president/past-presidents/

[lxxxiv] A&I posts enrollment decrease. (1986, September 19). Corpus Christi Caller.

[lxxxv] Rosser, J. (1978, October 12). CCSU worker must move after years on campus. Corpus Christi Caller, p. 66.

[lxxxvi] Lochbaum, P. (1979, April 4). Area colleges discourage foreign students. Corpus Christi Caller, p. 19.

[lxxxvii] Ozio, R. (1977, August 21). Classes to begin Aug. 29 at Corpus Christi State. Corpus Christi Caller, p. 23.

[lxxxviii] University of Corpus Christi plans huge expansion pro gram. (1953,June 7). Dallas Morning News.

[lxxxix] Wrotenbery, C. R. (1998). Baptist Island College. Fort Worth, Texas: Eakin Press.

[xc] Early Childhood Development Center. (2020, August 27). Texas A&M University Corpus Christi. https://ecdc.tamucc.edu/

[xci] Moore Foundation. (2020). https://moorefoundationcc.com/

[xcii] Halladay, D. W. (1972, December 31). Texas A&I-CC plans to be flexible, original in scope. Corpus Christi Caller-Times, p. 81.

[xciii] 217 receive degrees at CCSU commencement. (1980, December 19). Corpus Christi Caller, p. 23.

[xciv] Lopez, A. (2016, February 23). Rodriguez Honored by LULAC. Nueces County Record Star. https://www.recordstar.com/article/20160223/NEWS/160229733

[xcv] University panel to study tenure. (1982, March 12). Corpus Christi Caller, p. 23.

[xcvi] Goodwin, B. (1983, July 15). Leach: Laredo State will not 'dis appear'. Corpus Christi Caller, p. 22.

[xcvii] Palmer, D. (1987, April 16). Unity cited as key to improving higher education. Corpus Christi Caller, p. 13.

[xcviii] History of the UT System. (2020, August 23). The University of Texas System. https://www.utsystem.edu/offices/chancellor/history-ut-system

[xcix] Hunter, C. A., & Hunter, L. G. (2000). Texas A&M University Kingsville. Charleston, SC: Arcadia.

[c] Dietz, K. (1993, June 1). CCSU, A&I stand to benefit from legislative priorities. Corpus Christi Caller-Times, A5.

[ci] Halladay, D. W. (1972, December 31). Texas A&I-CC plans to be flexible, original in scope. Corpus Christi Caller-Times, p. 81.

[cii] Rosser, J. (1980, February 10). Enrollment drop worries Texas A&I. Corpus Christi Caller-Times, p. 15.

[ciii] Goodwin, B. (1987, November 11). Sugg says A&M, UT eyeing South Texas campuses. The Corpus Christi Caller-Times, p. 1.

[civ] Williams, L. (1987, May 15). Theory didn't work in Florida, Alan Sugg says. Corpus Christi Caller, p. 1.

[cv] Palmer, D. (1987, April 28). Merger of Del Mar, CCSU resurfaces. Corpus Christi Caller, p. 1.

[cvi] Thompson, J. (1990). Challenge and triumph: The first 20 years of Laredo State University. Laredo, Texas: Laredo State University.

[cvii] Palmer, D. (1987, April 16). Unity cited as key to improving higher education. Corpus Christi Caller, p. 13.

The Present

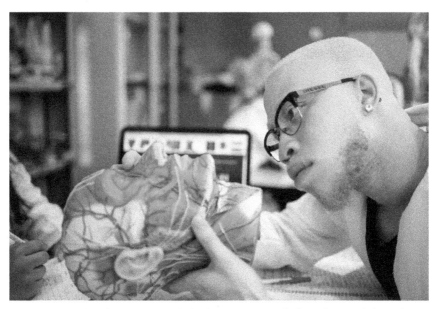

TAMU-CC Student Marcus Nkuko in Anatomy and Physiology Lab (2018)
Texas A&M University-Corpus Christi

In 1989, the Texas Legislature moved to merge the University System of South Texas into the Texas A&M University System (TAMUS). The Island University would again welcome freshman and sophomore students beginning in fall of 1994 as part of the transition to membership in the TAMUS.[i][ii] Joining these two systems would solidify TAMUS as the second largest university system in the state behind The University of Texas System.[iii] Before the merger, the Texas A&M University System consisted of Tarleton State University in Stephenville, Texas A&M University-College Station with a branch campus at Galveston, and Prairie View A&M University.[iv] The addition of the USST schools would increase the number of universities to six. This would be a considerable move forward and position TAMUS to continue its growth and footprint across Texas in future decades.

Kingsville President Steve Altman (1946-) had strongly lobbied for the three USST institutions to join TAMUS. A bill in 1987 expanding the USST had failed to pass. However, during the next legislative session in 1989, a bill merging the two systems was approved and signed into law by Governor Bill Clements (1917-2011) on May 26, 1989.[v] When signing the bill, Clements stated "Clearly these are watershed measures that will enhance quality education in South Texas. These bills symbolize our commitment to our youth and to their well-being."[vi]

The bill not only merged the three universities in the USST into the TAMUS, but it merged Pan American University, along with its Brownsville Campus, into the UT System.[vii] In 2013, UT would expand through the founding of UT Brownsville followed by a subsequent (re-)merger of these two institutions to form UT Rio Grande Valley. This institution would become home to a medical school alongside several teaching sites in the southernmost region of Texas.[viii]

Texas A&M University-Corpus Christi (TAMU-CC) would be situated in the largest city of any of the TAMUS universities. It was also somewhat unique in that many of the other schools had strong ties to agricultural education. The focus on marine sciences was more akin to the satellite campus in Galveston. The merger would mean that for the first time in its history, Corpus Christi would have a comprehensive university serving freshman through graduate students. Accordingly, the number of students living on-campus would increase dramatically. Facilities to meet the needs of the growing student body, from dining options to recreational activities, would greatly expand.

Campus Housing (2013)
Texas A&M University-Corpus Christi

The TAMU-CC atmosphere would again have elements that had been missing since the days of UCC as sports, student groups, fraternal organizations, housing and on-campus activities would be revived or gain prominence. The Island University would also continue to attract professionals and part-time students as it continued to expand offerings, particularly master's degrees. TAMU-CC would be poised to meet the needs of students from South Texas and around the world.

The leadership structure changed as TAMU-CC would be part of one of the largest university systems in the nation. The Chancellor of the System is based in College Station. Dr. Barry B. Thompson (1936-2014),[ix] would serve as Chancellor from 1994 to 1999. He had served as president of Tarleton State University and West Texas A&M University.

Dr. Barry B. Thompson (n.d.)
Tarleton State University

Howard Graves (1939-2003), A. Benton Cocanougher (interim) (1938-), Robert McTeer (1943-), Michael McKinney (1952-) and Jay Kimbrough (interim) (1948-2020) would serve in succession as Chancellor between 1999 and 2011.[x]

In September 2011, former Texas State Representative, Senator, and State Comptroller of Public Accounts John Sharp (1950-) would be named Chancellor.[xi] By 2021, the Texas A&M University System encompassed 11 universities and other state agencies including the Texas Division of Emergency Management, Forest Service, AgriLife Extension Service, Transportation Institute, and Health Science Center.[xii]

Texas A&M University System Chancellor John Sharp (2018)
Texas A&M University -Corpus Christi

President Dr. Robert R. Furgason
Texas A&M University-Corpus Christi

President Furgason

The Island University would also have a new leader as Dr. Robert R. Furgason was named president in December 1990.[xiii] Born in Spokane, Washington, Furgason came to CCSU from the University of Nebraska-Lincoln where he served as Vice Chancellor for Academic Affairs. The 55-year-old Furgason was selected out of a candidate pool of 160 applicants.

Furgason is an engineer with extensive international experience who speaks Spanish fluently. He had been a National Science Foundation consultant to the Escuela Politecnica Nacional in Quito, Ecuador where he lived for over a year. This experience included working with the Peace Corps and on projects for the U.S. Agency for International Development.[xiv]

One of the first acts Furgason undertook as president was to change the date on the University Seal to 1947.[xv] The date had been changed to 1973 when the university became a public institution, but the reversion back to 1947 signaled a sense of unity for all the students who had studied on the Island. This was important as some UCC alumni did not feel strong attachment to the public institution.

Furgason would lead the Island University for 14 years through an exceptional period of growth and change. When he began, there were 5,125 students enrolled at CCSU, and by the end of his tenure as president, TAMU-CC had 8,227 students. He oversaw $250 million in capital improvements. In this same period, Hispanic enrollments increased dramatically, as did scholarship awards and degree offerings. By 2004, 36 bachelor's degrees and 28 graduate degrees were offered across four colleges. This year would also mark the addition of a fifth college, the College of Nursing and Health Sciences. The university had operated with four colleges since its time as A&I.[xvi]

In the mid-1990s, efforts to bring a health science center to TAMU--CC were ultimately not successful.[xvii] This disappointment would again highlight the scarcity of professional schools in South Texas. Corpus Christi remains the largest city in Texas without easy access to a law, medical, dental, or veterinarian school.[xviii]

Marine Biology Research (2013)
Texas A&M University-Corpus Christi

In 1992, advanced studies did come to TAMU-CC in the form of a doctoral degree in Educational Leadership through a partnership with Texas A&M University-Kingsville. Jaye A. Mandt of Corpus Christi and Ken Stevenson of Beeville became the first students to receive doctoral degrees from TAMU-CC in 1995.[xix] Other doctoral programs followed, including a Doctor of Philosophy in Coastal and Marine Systems degree in 2003. This degree was the first doctoral degree to be offered by the College of Science and Engineering. [xx] A doctoral program in Curriculum and Instruction was started in 2004 to help address the need for teacher preparation in the region.[xxi]

Furgason would oversee a time of significant change as the Island University not only joined the TAMUS but transitioned from an upper-level institution to a comprehensive university offering freshman courses through doctoral degrees. He was fortunate to have significant support from the community. The "4 CCU" campaign supported the goal of expanding the Island University to a comprehensive institution. In addition to raising funds locally, the legislature allocated funding for campus upgrades in 1993 in the amount of $22 million issued as Tuition Revenue Bonds or TRBs. These funds would be used to provide significant infrastructure improvements, including a campus wide chiller system that cools water overnight to then regulate building temperatures during the day. This is accomplished through a closed loop system of underground pipes and the storage of chilled water in the iconic water tower on the south side of the campus. Roads and improvements to the bridge to the campus were also completed.[xxii]

ECDC Dedication Ceremony with President Furgason and State Representative Todd A. Hunter (1996)
Special Collections and Archives, Mary and Jeff Bell Library, Texas A&M University-Corpus Christi

TRBs as a financing mechanism would be an important source of funding for establishing TAMU-CC and TAMU-Kingsville. The use of the financing mechanism by the state has been expanded for use across all public institutions mainly for building new facilities and upgrades to existing facilities.[xxiii]

Gov. George W. Bush Visits the Early Childhood Development Center (1997)
Special Collections and Archives, Mary and Jeff Bell Library, Texas A&M University-Corpus Christi

Furgason was instrumental in a second fundraising effort with the launch of the 'Wave of the Future Capital Campaign' in 1997.[xxiv] As a result of these fundraising efforts, Furgason would oversee several large construction projects on campus. The $8 million Early Childhood Development Center (ECDC) was opened in 1996 for 88 Corpus Christi Independent School District Students. By its third year of operation, the center was designed to accommodate 132 students from age three to grade three.[xxv]

Expansion of on-campus housing, a $3 million dollar University Support Services facility, and the $12 million Center for Instruction were completed in the mid-1990s.[xxvi][xxvii] Governor George W. Bush visited the ECDC in October 1997 to support his commitment to childhood literacy. Bush stated of the center, "I see an intensive commitment to ensure that all children learn to read." During this visit, Bush discussed his re-election bid for Texas governor but also alluded to a potential run for U.S. President in 2000.[xxviii] Literacy would be an initiative President Bush would champion.

Students in the University Center (circa 2000)
Texas A&M University-Corpus Christi

In 1999, the University Center was constructed at a cost of $15.9 million. The UC provided 100,000 square feet of space for study areas, dining options, a bookstore, and offices. The facility replaced the woefully overcrowded Glasscock Student Center which had been built at a time when the campus had 800 students. The Glasscock building would be repurposed as a student success center.[xxix]

Construction of the MOMENTUM Sculpture (2003)
Texas A&M University-Corpus Christi

The MOMENTUM sculpture was erected in 2003 at the entrance to campus. Flanking Ocean Drive, the iconic stainless-steel structure features five spires and a wave shape measuring 30 feet in diameter. The wave sculpture summons a feeling of wind and water. According to the sculptor, the spires represent educational elements: Strength & Courage, Order, Movement, Accomplishment, and Logic. The spires are also representative of the five institutions in the history of the Island University. Each spire is 32 feet high and topped with a blue cobalt light. Light also emanates from the bottom of each spire to simulate the feeling they are floating at night. The spires represent stability in the face of the more turbulent wave portion of the installation. The use of indigenous landscaping, a curved retaining wall invoking a ship's curvature, and four-foot-tall lettering stating "Texas A&M University-Corpus Christi" complete the sculpture.

MOMENTUM was designed by artist Robert Roesch and approved by Furgason and local philanthropists Shirley "Sam" (1936-2008)[xxx] and William "Dusty" Durrill, (1934-2016)[xxxi] who underwrote the project. The monument was not only thought-provoking but was on a scope that fit the large open space at the entrance to campus. Roesch relied on six fine arts students to assist with construction. [xxxii]

Bay Hall was opened in fall of 2005. The building was still receiving finishing touches as students began class, but the classroom and office space were sorely needed.[xxxiii] The facility cost $15 million and was the largest academic building on campus with seating for 850 students across multiple lecture halls with a total of 63,000 square feet. Bay Hall would become home to several academic departments within the College of Arts and Humanities, now named the College of Liberal Arts.[xxxiv]

Bay Hall (2016)
Texas A&M University-Corpus Christi

One of the last projects started under Furgason was the Performing Arts Center, commonly known as the "PAC." The $18 million, 62,850-square-foot building was completed in 2005, and its prominent feature is the 1,500-person concert hall. Funding was provided through public and private funds, including a $3.5 million gift from Edward and Janet Harte.[xxxv] Samuel Frech, a Corpus Christi financial consultant, gave a $1 million gift toward the facility.[xxxvi] The remaining funding for the facility was secured through state issued tuition revenue bonds (TRBs) for $11 million.[xxxvii]

The facility faces Ocean Drive with an atrium that overlooks Corpus Christi Bay through an impressive four-story tall glass façade. In addition to numerous TAMU-CC performances, the PAC is home to the Corpus Christi Symphony and the Corpus Christi Chorale. Through the support of President Emeritus and Mrs. Furgason, the BRAVO! Series is an ongoing tribute to performers of the Coastal Bend.[xxxviii]

Construction of Performing Arts Center "PAC" (2004)
Special Collections and Archives, Mary and Jeff Bell Library, Texas A&M University-Corpus Christi

The architect for the PAC was Gordon E. Landreth of Cotton, Landreth, Kramer Architects and Associates Inc. in Corpus Christi. Landreth founded CLK Architects in 1977, and in addition to the PAC, he was the architect for expansion of the Corpus Christi Christus Spohn Health System and the memorial to the late Tejano singer Selena Quintanilla. In 2016, Landreth was named an outstanding alumnus of Texas A&M University-College Station.[xxxix]

Performing Arts Center
Texas A&M University -Corpus Christi

The New York City-based firm of Hardy, Holzman, Pfeiffer Architects consulted on design of the PAC. The sound quality in the PAC is world class, having been designed by Dr. J. Christopher Jaffe (1927-2013). Jaffee was an acclaimed acoustician and faculty member at the Juilliard School, City University of New York, and Rensselaer Polytechnic Institute. In addition to the PAC, he worked on over 250 performance venue projects including acoustic renovations of the Hollywood Bowl, Zankel Hall at Carnegie Hall, John F. Kennedy Center, Bass Performance Hall, Severance Hall, and Tokyo International Forum.[xl] Tejano artist Freddy Fender, world-renowned pianist Van Cliburn, violinists Itzhak Perlman and Joshua Bell, and Mezzo Soprano Frederica von Stade have all performed at the PAC. The facility was renovated in 2021.[xli]

Performing Arts Center
Texas A&M University- Corpus Christi

The Corpus Christi Symphony Orchestra Performs at the Performing Arts Center (n.d.)
Texas A&M University-Corpus Christi

Upon his retirement as President, Furgason did not leave the university but became the first executive director of the Harte Research Institute for Gulf of Mexico Studies in January 2005.[xlii] The HRI occupies a building at the entrance to the Island University on Ocean Drive just south of the iconic MOMENTUM sculpture.

Researchers from the Harte Research Institute of Gulf of Mexico Studies (2013)
Texas A&M University-Corpus Christi

In 2018, the Science and Technology Building was renamed the Dr. Robert R. Furgason Engineering Building in honor of the Island University's ninth president. President Emeritus Furgason arrived at the dedication ceremony in a teal 1958 Cadillac. He dynamically mingled with the numerous civic leaders and university supporters who were in attendance. The building is a 67,000-square-foot facility built in 2001 adjacent to the Center for Sciences.[xliii]

Dr. Robert R. Furgason Engineering Building (2020)
Andrew Johnson

When Furgason became director of the Harte Research Institute, he was overseeing the implementation of a visionary gift to TAMU-CC. Edward H. Harte (1922-2011) endowed the Harte Research Institute for Gulf Coast Studies (HRI) with a $46 million donation, the largest in the history of the Island University. The gift was to endow six faculty positions and their supporting graduate students to conduct research on the Gulf of Mexico. The gift also included $10 million for facility upgrades.[xliv] The HRI building was secured through state tuition revenue bonds issued in 2003.[xlv] The HRI would greatly expand the scope of ongoing work conducted by the Center for Coastal Studies and the Water Resource Center.[xlvi][xlvii]

The HRI engages in numerous projects to study the Gulf of Mexico. The institute is involved in oyster conservation, sea level studies, shark tracking, oil spill reclamation, the assessment of ecosystems, fisheries management, and many other projects. The endowed chairs of HRI represent a breadth of disciplines, including law and economics, that are reflective of the complexities involved with the study of the Gulf of Mexico.

Some of the most widely known work of the HRI is on the study of sharks. HRI scientists continue to be regularly featured on the popular television series "Shark Week" on the Discovery Channel. The show has led to local community programs by HRI to increase awareness about the Gulf's ecosystems and HRI research.[xlix]

Diver with the Harte Research Institute for Gulf Coast Studies (n.d.)
Texas A&M University-Corpus Christi

The HRI is a leader in studying the effects of the 2010 Deepwater Horizon Oil Spill, which occurred in the Gulf waters off the coast of Mississippi. Deepwater Horizon is widely considered the worst oil spill in history. Through a coalition of institutions in the Texas ONE GULF Center of Excellence, HRI scientists have studied the long-term effects of this disaster to better understand the resilience of ecosystems. To this end, in 2017, TAMU-CC was designated as a RESTORE Research Center of Excellence.[l] The six endowed chairs, with expertise in a broad range of areas, allows HRI to study the Gulf from numerous perspectives and pivot to address challenges as they arise.

Ed Harte (n.d.)
Texas A&M University-Corpus Christi

Harte had a background that gave him a thorough understanding of the Gulf of Mexico. An acclaimed writer and newspaper publisher, he was well-versed in Mexico-U.S. relations. Thus, he understood that studying the Gulf of Mexico would require participation of the U.S., Mexico, and Cuba--an idea that is reflected in the organization and operation of HRI. Members of the advisory council for the HRI are from each of these nations.[xlviii]

Harte was a publisher of newspapers including the *Corpus Christi Caller-Times,* prior to his retirement in 1987. A strong advocate for environmental protection, Harte served on the American Farmland Trust board and was a board member and chairman of the National Audubon Society. Harte was instrumental in protecting Padre Island by securing its status as a national seashore for 67 miles of coastline. He sought protection for an additional 4,000 acres of coastline by having it designated as Mustang Island State Park. Along with his brother, Houston, they donated 66,000 acres in West Texas to Big Bend National Park to become the North Rosillos Mountains Preserve.[li][lii]

President Killebrew

Dr. Flavius C. Killebrew (1949-), a quiet and reserved, yet formidable Professor of Zoology, became TAMU-CC President in 2005. Killebrew had served at Texas A&M University-West Texas in Canyon as Provost and Vice-President of Academic Affairs. During his tenure, capital expansion totaling $350 million occurred on the Island University. Under Killebrew, the university raised $62 million in donations and saw an increase in student enrollment of 36%. He would oversee several major construction projects as well as begin a nearby campus addition.[liii]

In his first year, Killebrew set out a 10-year strategic plan named Momentum 2015.[liv] The plan called for increasing research, faculty profiles, and student admission requirements. Additional points in the plan addressed the importance of community engagement, alumni involvement, and attracting a diverse community of faculty, staff, and students. In 2006, Killebrew would note that growth of TAMU-CC would require additional space.[lv]

In support of this vision, several new degree options would be added. These programs included six new doctoral degrees including

President Dr. Flavius Killebrew
Texas A&M University-Corpus Christi

Marine Science and Geospatial Surveying. Mechanical Engineering was also offered as an undergraduate program beginning in 2010. In addition to the state funding necessary to begin the degree, the program garnered broad community support in the form of scholarships and matching funds, including a $2 million infusion from the Corpus Christi Business and Job Development Corporation. Large segments of the Corpus Christi economy, such as petroleum refining and heavy industry, rely on engineering expertise. Engineering degrees are costly to start due to the specialized classroom lab space and equipment needed for instruction.[lvi]

Killebrew's push for additional research activity resulted in increased expenditure for research from $16 million in 2013 to $25 million in 2015.[lvii] Much of this increase in research expenditure is due to the work of the Harte Research Institute. In 2018, the university would be designated as an 'R2: Doctoral Universities - High Research Activity' under the Carnegie Classification system for Universities. This distinction reflects a faculty that is increasingly engaged in research and in particular projects that are funded externally such as by the National Science Foundation (NSF) and other government sources. Despite these successes, Killebrew was unable to add programs in occupational therapy, physical therapy, and architecture.[lviii]

President Dr. Flavius Killebrew (2016)
Texas A&M University-Corpus Christi

During Killebrew's 12 years as president, the campus underwent several major physical upgrades. He would oversee the addition of Island Hall and the Dr. Jack and Susie Dugan Wellness Center. These structures were built southwest of the existing field house and swimming pool. The Dugan Wellness Center is a 67,000-square-foot, $21 million facility featuring basketball courts, a fitness center, offices for athletics and recreational sports, locker rooms, and group exercise rooms. This facility replaced the Glasscock Fitness and Wellness Center, a 6,200-square-foot facility built in 1968.[lix][lx] In 2007, students narrowly approved a fee increase, by just 12 votes, to pay for a portion of the Dugan Wellness Center and its ongoing operations.[lxi] Adjacent to the Dugan Wellness Center, Island Hall is a 148,000-square-foot building that is home to the College of Nursing and Health Sciences and the College of Education's kinesiology program. The $45 million facility has an indoor track, classroom space, offices, laboratory space, and a state-of the-art biomechanics laboratory.[lxii]

Dr. Jack and Susie Dugan Wellness Center (n.d.)
Texas A&M University-Corpus Christi

Participants in the Emergency Care Workshop (2018)
Texas A&M University-Corpus Christi

Students in Corpus Christi Bay Near Campus (2019)
Texas A&M University-Corpus Christi

In 2010, TAMU-CC opened the Woo Sung Lee Alumni Welcome Center on Ennis Joslin Drive overlooking the island campus.[lxiii] Woo Sung Lee was an alumnus of UCC. He also generously donated to scholarships and funds to construct Lee Plaza.[lxiv] The plaza, with its fountain, outdoor seating, and attractive landscaping, provides a place for students to gather. Lee Plaza is centered between the O'Connor Building, Corpus Christi Hall, the round building, and the campus Welcome Center.[lxv] Lee Plaza is the site for several momentous events each year. The area is extensively decorated for the Holiday season and features a Christmas Tree. Lee Plaza serves as the centerpiece for the university's Holiday celebration. Following the ring ceremony, students come to Lee Plaza to participate in the "The Islander Ring Wish" tradition by tossing a sand dollar into the fountain to make a wish about the future.[lxvi]

Woo Sung Lee Alumni Welcome Center
(2012)
Texas A&M University-Corpus Christi

The Plaza is a tribute to Lee's late son, Yongnam Lee, and serves as a memorial to other students as well. During the spring, the Islander Tribute is held in Lee Plaza to remember any student lost during the preceding year.[lxvii] Pavers feature the names of students who have passed away while attending TAMU-CC. As of 2021, there were 82 inscribed bricks in honor of students. A statement above the pavers reads "Let us not forget our fellow Islanders."

A Campus Tour Group Outside the Islander Welcome Center (n.d.)
Texas A&M University-Corpus Christi

Lee Plaza During the Holidays (2016)
Texas A&M University-Corpus Christi

The Michael and Karen O'Connor building was completed in 2011. Karen O'Connor was instrumental in funding the building through a $6 million gift towards the $25 million cost of the facility.[lxviii][lxix] The gift honored her late husband, Michael, who passed in 2003 from a rare, incurable blood cancer. In addition to her philanthropic support of and advocacy for TAMU-CC, Karen O'Connor Urban has worked to advance healthcare in South Texas among other charitable pursuits.[lxx]

Michael and Karen O'Connor Building (2020)
Andrew Johnson

Michael A. O'Connor (1935-2003) attended Notre Dame University and was a heavy-weight boxing champion. He ultimately graduated from St. Edward's University in Austin, Texas with a business administration degree in 1958. He moved to Corpus Christi to work for the Gardner-Denver Company, a manufacturer of pumps and compressors. O'Connor would begin several successful businesses and his career would culminate as Chairman of the Board of Directors at Hanover Compressor Company. Under his guidance, the company would be come a publicly traded company on the New York Stock Exchange in 1997.[lxxi]

President Dr. Furgason, Karen O'Connor, Michael O'Connor,
College of Business Dean Dr. Moustafa H. Abdelsamad
*Special Collections and Archives, Mary and Jeff Bell Library, Texas
A&M University-Corpus Christi*

Students Julie Williams, Stephen Gibson, and Blake Cox Study in the Michael and
Karen O'Connor Building (2017)
Texas A&M University-Corpus Christi

The 75,000-square-foot O'Connor Building houses faculty and administrative offices of the College of Business in addition to computer labs, study areas, classrooms, and meeting spaces. A real-time stock ticker runs the width of the main lobby facing the east entrance of the building.

The Momentum Campus is a 156-acre site located off Ennis Joslin Drive and Nile Drive donated to TAMU-CC by the City of Corpus Christi in 2008. The site was previously used by the city for sports fields. This new campus began with the construction of the Thomas J. Henry Tennis Center, located off Nile Drive. The $2.4 million facility opened in 2011 and has 12 NCAA regulation courts. Henry is a prominent attorney and supporter of Islander Athletics.[lxxii] A track and soccer pitch would be added in 2013 with support from the Dugan family.

Dr. Jack A. Dugan is a respected ophthalmologist and rated as one of the nation's top 100 eye surgeons. Following a residency at the University of Texas and service as the Chief of Eye Surgery at Fort Benning, Georgia during the Vietnam War, Dugan moved to Corpus Christi. He started the Dugan Eye Institute of Corpus Christi in 1977. The Dugan Family has given generously to support athletics and recreational sports at the Island University.[lxxiii]

Thomas J. Henry Tennis Center (n.d.)
Texas A&M University-Corpus Christi

Thomas J. Henry Tennis Center (n.d.)
Texas A&M University-Corpus Christi

Dugan Family Soccer Complex (2013)
Texas A&M University-Corpus Christi

Momentum Village student housing is located on Ennis Joslin Drive. The first phase was completed in 2015 and housed 482 students. The units were leased at full capacity in the semester in which they opened and planning for construction of a second phase was undertaken immediately.[lxxiv] The second phase was begun on July 6, 2016 and opened for fall 2017 classes. This opening would add an additional 560 beds to bring the total capacity of Momentum Village to 1,042 students. The total capacity for all student housing with these additions was 2,832 students in 2017. The Momentum Campus is notable in that it increased the physical footprint of the campus allowing facilities that require large tracks of land, such as sports venues, to be constructed. This arrangement allows for instructional and research facilities to be prioritized on Ward Island while still allowing for campus expansion.[lxxv]

Momentum Village Student Housing (2015)
Texas A&M University-Corpus Christi

With the increased emphasis as a residential campus, a food truck was added on campus in 2013 while a new dining hall was opened in 2014. The 18,700-square-foot facility has seating for 400 and features numerous food options. In 2019, the dining hall was designated as an 'Ocean Friendly' restaurant for its green initiatives such as the reduction of food packaging. The university introduced a related measure deploying eco friendly waste bins to promote sustainability.[lxxvi]

An important program was solidified under Killebrew. The TAMU--CC Reserve Officers' Training Corps (ROTC) program began as the Javelina Battalion's Charlie Company (Kingsville) in 1978 with the U.S. Army. In 2006, the TAMU-CC Islander Army ROTC was formed and is organized within the Military Science Department of the College of Education and Human Development.

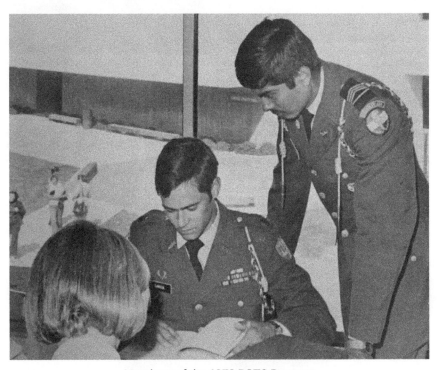

Members of the 1978 ROTC Program
Special Collections and Archives, Mary and Jeff Bell Library, Texas A&M University-Corpus Christi

ROTC Rock Climbing (n.d.)
*Special Collections and Archives, Mary and Jeff Bell Library, Texas
A&M University-Corpus Christi*

A Welcome Center was added alongside Lee Plaza in 2013 to greet prospective students. The center allows students to complete admissions applications and arrange for campus tours. Killebrew would also oversee a 35,000-square-foot expansion of the University Center in 2015 at a cost of $27.5 million.[lxxvii]

Construction of Tidal Hall, a new $60 million, 111,000-square-foot Life Science and Engineering Building, would begin in August 2016 and open in 2019. The building features classrooms, nine teaching labs, 34 research labs, and 100 offices. Funding from the project was mostly provided by the State of Texas using tuition revenue bonds approved in 2015.[lxxviii]

Tidal Hall (2020)
Andrew Johnson

Students Work in a Lab in Tidal Hall (2020)
Texas A&M University-Corpus Christi

Killebrew would serve the TAMUS in various capacities for 43 years. Immediately following his retirement as president, he worked to advise the Lone Star UAS Center of Excellence and Innovation.[lxxix] He was awarded the title of "President Emeritus" in 2017 by the TAMUS Board of Regents.

Student Body President Garrett Ransom, Vice-President Andrea Gilson with Dr. and Mrs. Killebrew (2018)
Texas A&M University-Corpus Christi

President Kelly Miller with TAMU-CC Students (n.d.).
Texas A&M University-Corpus Christi

President Kelly Miller

Dr. Kelly M. Miller began at the Island University as an Assistant Professor of Communication in 1994. Her entire academic career has been spent at TAMU-CC rising through the ranks as a Department Chair, Director of the School of Arts, Media & Communication, Dean of the College of Liberal Arts, and as Provost and Vice-President of Academic Affairs. Miller holds a PhD in Communication from Pennsylvania State University. She has been a part of the Island University since the faculty was expanded to accommodate the return of freshman students to the university. Accordingly, Miller knows the campus, faculty, and community well.[lxxx] While serving as Provost, Miller was selected to serve as interim President upon the retirement of Killebrew in December 2016. In August 2017, she was selected to fill the role on a permanent basis.[lxxxi]

President Miller with Students During her Surprise Birthday Party (2018)
Texas A&M University-Corpus Christi

Reception for State Legislative Delegation (2017). President Dr. Kelly Miller, State Senator Juan "Chuy" Hinojosa, State Representative Todd Hunter
Texas A&M University-Corpus Christi

President Miller joined the Island University at a time of important change as lower division courses were again offered. She has spent her entire academic career on the Island:

> *I joined Texas A&M University-Corpus Christi on August 24, 1994 as an assistant professor. I had just graduated from arguably the top communication program in the country at that time, moved thousands of miles away from home, and the campus resembled an outdated army barracks in many places.*
>
> *So then, why did I choose the Island University? Because from the first moment I stepped foot on the island, -it was electric. The energy was contagious. And there was a vision, a bold vision, that we were determined to achieve. We were determined to close the gap in educational attainment and help first generation, low-income students become successful professionals and leaders in Texas.*
>
> *Twenty-seven years later, I can honestly say Texas A&M University-Corpus Christi is by all accounts a true success story. We have grown in enrollment, in research, in prestige, and in supporting economic development for our region, but we have never lost sight of what makes this campus truly special - our unparalleled commitment to student success.*
>
> *-President Kelly M. Miller, 2021[lxxxiz]*

Miller would face a series of major events beginning as soon as she was named interim President. The 2017 Legislative Session proved to be eventful for higher education in the Coastal Bend Region as a push to merge TAMU-CC and Texas A&M University-Kingsville took place. Broadly speaking, the proposal would have created a single A&M university from the two independent campuses.[lxxxiii] The measure was designed to cut costs by consolidating functions between the two campuses that are located less than 40 miles apart. At the time, Kingsville was experiencing declines in enrollment and associated financial difficulties. The proposal would have merged administrations, student services, and programs to better realize economies of scale and efficiencies. Some details were not included in the proposal, such as the name of the would-be institution, location of the headquarters, any changes to programs or degrees, the continuation of sports, and the mascot.

The proposal was met with resistance from both the Corpus Christi and Kingsville communities and many alumni from both universities. Concerns ranged from the use of one mascot over the other, the loss of programs, and the location of the main administrative offices. The allocation of resources to campuses and the location of the chief administrators had also been constant points of contention under the USST administrative structure. Ultimately, the proposal did not move forward when members of the Corpus Christi area state legislative delegation joined State Representative J. M. Lozano (Kingsville) in withholding support for the measure by not filing enabling legislation.[lxxxiv]

Another storm rocked the campus in 2017. Hurricane Harvey, a Category 4 storm, made landfall north of Corpus Christi at San Jose Island on August 26, 2017. The storm quickly intensified from a tropical depression to a major hurricane while in the Gulf of Mexico. Miller was confirmed by the Texas A&M University System Board of Regents to fill the presidency on a permanent basis on the same day that campus was closed in advance of the storm. She would return to campus as soon as the vote was held to lead the response to the hurricane.

Hurricane Harvey caused an estimated $125 billion in damage to Texas and southwest Louisiana. Strong winds damaged the Island University, particularly to the roofs of several buildings. Major flooding was present on the barrier islands and areas north of Corpus Christi, particularly affecting the Houston Metropolitan Region. Many Islanders were displaced as the campus had mandatory evacuations while much of the region had recommended evacuations. Some students, faculty, and staff lost their homes in the storm, thus making the academic year challenging for many. Restoration of electricity took several days for parts of Corpus Christi while parts of the region sustained more considerable infrastructure damage. The storm made landfall two days before classes were to begin, thus causing a delay. TAMU-CC employees returned to work on August 30 and classes began on September 5, 2017.[lxxxv]

TAMU-CC Students Assist Members of the Community During the BIG Event Day of Service (2018)
Texas A&M University-Corpus Christi

Islanders would meet the challenges caused by Harvey head-on. Almost immediately, groups of students began helping to rebuild area communities. Students removed debris and fallen trees in the hard-hit community of Rockport. The BIG Event held in April 2018 included 1,000 student volunteers contributing more than 4,000 hours focusing on neighborhoods that sustained hurricane damage. The effort to better prepare the Gulf Region for hurricanes is ongoing with TAMU-CC researchers assisting businesses and communities not only with recovery efforts but to become more resilient in the event of another major storm.[lxxxvi]

While Miller is not the first 'President Miller' of the Island University, she is the first female President. During Miller's tenure, several women would serve in prominent administrative roles. Among these appointments was Dr. Clarenda Phillips who was named Provost and Vice-President of Academic Affairs in March 2018.[lxxxvii] The increased diversity in faculty, staff, and administration is more reflective of the make-up of the student body. In 2019, 6,953 female students attended TAMU-CC or 60.7% of the total student body.[lxxxviii]

President Miller with Students at Women's Basketball Game (2019)
Dr. Kenneth Iyescas

Miller has indicated that she looks forward to a time when women being promoted to leadership positions is not an exceptional event. Indeed, her administration has broken a glass ceiling and advanced the Island University as an increasingly diverse place to learn and work.[lxxxix]

Dr. Martin Luther King Jr. Day March (2003)
Special Collections and Archives, Mary and Jeff Bell Library, Texas A&M University-Corpus Christi

The student body is diverse with, 5% being Black, 48% Hispanic, 37% White, 3% Asian, and 5% other ethnicities in 2018. This is a significant change from the early decades of UCC when Sidney Smith (1944-2009) was the first African American UCC student. He attended during the 1960s and earned a Bachelor of Arts degree. He later earned a Master of Religious Education degree from Golden Gate Baptist Theological Seminary in Mill Valley, California in 1968, and a Ph.D. from California Graduate School of Theology in Glendale in 1973. Smith was the first director of the Florida Baptist Convention's African American ministries division serving from 1994-2005. Altogether, Smith served more than 40 years in Southern Baptist denominational roles and supported the opening of more than 400 congregations.[xc]

Another notable change is that TAMU-CC is now the educational home for students from across the nation, and around the world. CCSU only had 14 foreign students in 1979,[xci] a reflection of the focus on recruitment within the local area.[xcii] In the 2018-2019 academic year, international students from 55 different countries comprised 3% of the TAMU-CC student body.[xciii]

Sixty-five students from Vietnam, 53 from India, and 34 from China comprised the largest international groups by nation.[xciv] The Office of International Education assists these students and provides programing to promote understanding of other cultures among the campus community. One of their hallmark events is International Education Week held annually in late fall. Cultural presentations, international foods, discussions by Fulbright Scholars, a fashion show, and study abroad fair are among the activities held during this event.

Student Performance at the Performing Arts Center (n.d.)
Texas A&M University-Corpus Christi

Students Perform During the Colombian Carnival (2016)
Texas A&M University-Corpus Christi

President Miller and Students Perform During International Education Week (2019)
Texas A&M University -Corpus Christi

Students Perform During International Education Week (2019)
Texas A&M University-Corpus Christi

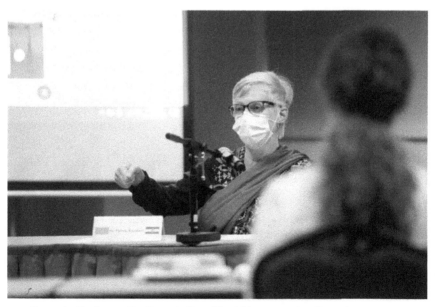

Regents Professor Dr. Pamela Brouillard Discusses her Experiences as a Fulbright Scholar (2020)
Texas A&M University-Corpus Christi

TAMU-CC is one of the most ethnically-diverse universities in Texas. Several programs recognize and build on this diversity. There is a long-standing center for bilingual education studies offering a minor in Spanish-English Translation and a certification in Teaching English to Speakers of Other Languages (TESOL)/Applied Linguistics. The College of Education offers a graduate level certification program in Counseling Spanish Speaking Clients. The College of Liberal Arts offers minors in Mexican American, Latin-American, and Women, Gender, and Sexuality Studies.[xcv]

TAMU-CC Art Student Jamie Gonzalez (2016)
Texas A&M University-Corpus Christi

Diversity initiatives also include events centered on Hispanic Heritage Month beginning each September 15 and lasting to October 15. Events including food, music, dance, and presentations on research and initiatives that impact the Hispanic community are held at this time.

To serve this diverse student body, Miller has made student graduation an important goal. This goal aligns with strategies set forth by the State but are particularly important given the large number of first-generation students served by the Island University. In 2019, half of the student body indicated they were first-generation college students.[xcvi] Miller's initiatives involve additional focus on student support, whether providing tutoring or adequate financial resources.[xcvii] Student success is a broad goal that involves processes from recruitment of prospective students through maintaining relationships with alumni who may return to the Island to serve as mentors. This strategy involves all stakeholders as faculty and advisors must be vested as well.

The university also projects its influence globally. In 1987, Dr. Wes Tunnell became the first faculty member from the Island University to be selected as a Fulbright scholar. Since the late 1980s, an impressive list of nine faculty have conducted research, taught, and consulted in a foreign nation as part of the prestigious Faculty Exchange Program.[xcviii]

Dr. Wes Tunnell Named As Fulbright Scholar

One of the most prestigiuous programs for professors studying and teaching abroad has named Dr. John "Wes" Tunnell a Fulbright Scholar.

A professor of biology, Tunnell is the first faculty member here to be designated a Fulbright Scholar. Dr. Robert Bezdek, associate professor of political science, received a Fulbright Scholarship prior to joining the CCSU faculty.

The international scholarship program for educational and cultural exchange will allow Tunnell to teach and do research in Mexico during the coming academic year.

He will lecture on his specialties of mollusk biology and coral and marine ecology at a relatively new education and research center in Merida on the northern Yucatan peninsula.

Tunnell has taught biology at CCSU since 1974, and helped spearhead the establishment of the Center for Coastal Studies during the past year.

With encouragement from other faculty members, Tunnell applied to the Fulbright program more than a year ago to fulfill an earlier invitation to teach at the four-year-old Yucatan center.

Tunnell admits he had almost forgotten about his application when the letter arrived telling him he had been awarded the Fulbright Scholarship.

Beyond the coming academic year, Tunnell plans to remain in Mexico next summer and perhaps join research on a coral atoll in the Caribbean Sea.

Article Announcing Dr. Tunnell's Fulbright Scholarship (1987)
Alumni Update, Summer 1987. Special Collections and Archives, Mary and Jeff Bell Library, Texas A&M University-Corpus Christi

Texas A&M University-Corpus Christi Fulbright Scholars

Dr. Wes Tunnell	Professor of Biology	Mexico	1987-1988
Mr. Louis Katz	Professor of Art	Thailand	1988-1989
Mr. Richard McLaughlin	Professor of Public Policy	Japan	1991-1992
Dr. Nancy Sullivan	Professor of English	Hong Kong	2001-2002
Dr. Kevin Concannon	Associate Professor of English	Germany	2002-2003
Dr. Jennifer Epley Sanders	Associate Professor of Political Science	Indonesia	2006
Dr. Karen Middleton	Professor of Management	Taiwan	2009-2010
Dr. Dorothy McClellan	Regents Professor of Criminal Justice	Croatia	2002-2004
Dr. Pamela Brouillard	Regents Professor of Psychology	Croatia	2004-2005
Dr. Pamela Brouillard	Regents Professor of Psychology	Kazakhstan	2014

Many talented faculty have taught at the Island University. Students learn skills and gain knowledge from their experiences inside and outside of the class room. Lives are often shaped by a "favorite professor" or faculty who challenge students to reach their full potential. Experiences from the years spent learning at a university have a profound impact for the rest of a student's life.

Dr. Wendi Pollock During a Mock Crime Scene Demonstration in the Faculty Center (2019)
Texas A&M University-Corpus Christi

Dr. Kenneth Iyescas Conducts a Band Class in the Center for Arts (2016)
Texas A&M University-Corpus Christi

The Texas A&M University System honors some of the most talented professors with the Regents Professor Award. One TAMU-CC faculty member has received this award each year since 1997.[xcix]

Regents Professor Dr. Awni Zebda Lectures on Cost Accounting (2017)
Texas A&M University-Corpus Christi

Texas A&M University-Corpus Christi Regents Professors

Dr. John "Wes" Tunnell	Professor of Biology	1997
Dr. Jane Wilhour	Professor of Education	1998
Dr. Richard E. Sheppard	Professor of Education	1999
Dr. Philip W. Rhoades	Professor of Criminal Justice	2000
Dr. C. Alan Berkebile	Professor of Geology	2001
Dr. Robert R. Bezdek	Professor of Political Science	2002
Dr. Leon Dube	Professor of Marketing	2003
Mr. Mark W. Anderson	Professor of Art	2004
Dr. Dorothy S. McClellan	Professor of Criminal Justice	2005
Dr. Suzzette F. Chopin	Professor of Biomedical Sciences	2006
Dr. Robert Wooster	Professor of History	2008
Dr. Awni M. Zebda	Professor of Accounting	2009
Dr. Robb Jackson	Haas Professor of English	2010
Dr. Pamela S. Meyer	Professor of Sociology	2011
Dr. Jim Lee	Professor of Economics	2012
Dr. Bryant Griffith	Professor of Education	2013
Dr. Donald R. Deis	Professor and Joslin Endowed Chair of Accounting	2014
Dr. Paul A. Montagna	Endowed Chair and Professor	2015
Dr. Marilyn Spencer	Professor of Economics	2016
Dr. Pamela J. Brouillard	Professor of Psychology	2017
Dr. Robert L. Smith	Professor of Counseling and Educational Psychology	2018
Dr. Elizabeth Sefcik	Professor of Nursing and Health Sciences	2019
Dr. Gregory W. Stunz	Professor of Marine Biology and Endowed Chair	2020

Under Miller, the push for higher levels of research expenditure continued. In 2018, she noted that at $28 million, Corpus Christi had the second highest level of research activity in the system, behind TAMU--College Station. New programs in Civil and Industrial Engineering were added due in part to the allocation of special item funding during the 2019 legislative session.[c]

TAMU-CC has expanded into online learning. The College of Business began offering courses as part of existing 'traditional' degree programs to then offer students the ability to complete the last two years of a bachelor's degree in a fully online format by 2018. This option is attractive to students who are completing two-year associate degree

programs at community colleges. The college also offers a Master of
Business Administration (MBA) and Master of Accountancy (MAcc)
programs in a fully online format. In 2020, the MBA program enrolled
over 1,000 students from across the U.S. and Canada. The College of
Nursing and Health Sciences offers an online Master of Science in Nursing degree for nurses who want to become Family Nurse Practitioners.
Other colleges also expanded into the online classroom. Offering online
degree offerings mean that students can access educational opportunities virtually anywhere in the world.[ci]

College of Business Students Studying in the O'Connor Building (2018)
Texas A&M University-Corpus Christi

In 2018, TAMU-CC joined with other TAMUS universities to
launch a unique educational opportunity for students in the Bryan,
Texas area. The RELLIS Campus is an initiative launched by TAMUS
Chancellor Sharp to extend the reach of system schools into the Brazos
Valley Region. While this region is home to TAMU-College Station, the
exceptional growth this university has experienced has led to an unfilled
need. Sharp indicated that RELLIS is an "academic alternative for students who want to live in Bryan-College Station but who for whatever

reason do not attend Texas A&M University [College Station]."[cii] Specifically, this could mean working professionals, or students who are seeking a specific major but do not meet the entrance requirements to be accepted into the program at College Station. Other degree programs, such as criminal justice, are offered at RELLIS by a system institution but not available at TAMU-College Station. Further, the cost of attendance at RELLIS is lower than at TAMU-College Station.

College of Business Dean Dr. John Gamble Congratulates an MBA Graduate in the Commencement Ceremony (August 8, 2015)
Texas A&M University-Corpus Christi

The RELLIS campus is located west of Bryan on State Highway 47. The 2,000-acre property was formerly the Bryan Army Airfield and was dedicated on June 6, 1943.[ciii][civ] Similarly, to Chase Field, Cuddihy Field, and Ward Island, the base was surplused by the U.S. Government following its use in World War II and the Korean conflict.

In 1962, TAMU-College Station began a similar arrangement as pursued by UCC to acquire the Ward Island property. After a 20-year lease agreement, the U.S. Government would transfer ownership to TAMU-College Station if the base was productively used as a campus. The property was renamed Riverside Campus in 1988 following the acquisition of the property. The Riverside campus provided an expansion opportunity at a time when the main campus was growing rapidly, particularly for research testing that required a large amount of space.[cv]

RELLIS Campus Entrance Sign (n.d.)
Texas A&M University System

The Riverside Campus was renamed the RELLIS Campus in 2015 to reflect the six Aggie (TAMU-College Station) core tenants: respect, excellence, leadership, loyalty, integrity and selfless service.[cvi] This change coincided with the acquisition of the campus from TAMU-College Station by the TAMUS and development of a master plan. The plan includes extensive research centers that build on the existing campus activities.[cvii] The Texas Transportation Institute has its headquarters and several testing facilities, the Texas A&M Engineering Experiment Station (TEES), Texas A&M Engineering Extension Service (TEEX), and a joint project between these two entities, the Center for Infrastructure Renewal are all located at RELLIS.[cviii] The TAMUS George H. W Bush Combat Development Complex (BCDC) is scheduled to be operational in 2021 and will be a testing center for emerging technologies used by the U.S. Army.[cix]

Part of the campus master plan includes the academic alliance, a center with degrees offered by system members from across the state. The arrangement is unique as students may take courses from different universities on the same campus. The RELLIS Campus alliance is predicated on a partnership with Blinn College, as the institution charged with offering core classes that comprise the first two years of a bachelor's degree.[ex] On-campus research partnerships allow for students to gain hands-on experience. Students are counted as attending their respective system university however, shared services such as library services, computer labs, and student engagement are handled by staff employed by the TAMUS.[cxi]

On the RELLIS Campus, TAMU-CC offered four Bachelor of Business Administration degree programs beginning in fall 2018. At launch, the TAMU-CC College of Business had the largest number of students in the inaugural semester with 66 students taught by three full--time faculty and supplemented by several adjunct instructors. The program has expanded in offerings and faculty and is experiencing a steady growth in the student body. By fall 2019, 177 TAMU-CC College of Business students were attending the RELLIS Campus taught by seven full-time and additional adjunct faculty.[cxii]

In 2019, the Island University established a presence in downtown Corpus Christi with the opening of the new Islanders Pavilion and Courts. This same year, TAMU-CC purchased a five-story building located on North Chaparral Street. Formerly occupied by retailer J.C. Penney, the 77,000-square-foot building was purchased for $2.3 million from Janet and Ernest "Buz" Maxwell. The building was built in 1947, the same year that UCC was founded. Renovation work and planning for the building began following the purchase. The building will provide a more direct link to the Corpus Christi community.[cxiii]

University of Corpus Christi Students Parade Past the J.C.
Penney Co. Building in Downtown Corpus Christi (Circa
1960s)
Mary and Jeff Bell Library, Special Collections and Archives
Department, Texas A&M University-Corpus Christi

President Miller and TAMU-CC faced another critical challenge in
2020 as the year was marked by the COVID-19 pandemic. Upon resumption of classes after spring break in March 2020, courses shifted to
an online only format for the remainder of the semester. At the height
of the pandemic, the campus would transition fully to online courses.
During this semester TAMU-CC faculty and staff pulled together and
managed to successfully assist 97% of students in completing the semester, outperforming other semesters. [cxv]

COVID-19 related signage in Corpus
Christi Hall (2020)
Andrew Johnson

Almost all summer courses were held online to allow for the campus to prepare for students, staff, and faculty to return in the fall of 2020. Social distancing and facial covering guidelines were set in place. Classrooms and offices were retrofitted with plexiglass shielding and signage to help lessen the contact among people in common areas. The fall 2020 semester offered more "hybrid" and online courses to lower the amount of traffic on-campus and allow for fewer people to be present in classrooms at one time. Across campus, precautions were taken by limiting congregation, offering COVID-19 testing, and through the placement of additional hand sanitizer and cleaning stations. Signage reminding students, faculty, and staff to "Protect the Island" was displayed across campus. Traffic in hallways, classrooms, and common areas was notably lower during the 2020-2021 academic year due to the implementation of social distancing guidelines.[cxvi]

Miller's time as president has been punctuated by major events. Even still, she is overseeing the growth of programs, facilities, and the broadening of research and community outreach. Her key initiatives are student-centered with an emphasis placed on being successful during college and well-prepared to enter the workforce or take the next step in their educational pursuits upon graduation.

**Provost and Vice President for Academic Affairs Dr.
Clarenda Phillips Congratulates Recent Graduates During a
"Drive-Thru Diploma Pickup" Event (Fall 2020)**
Texas A&M University-Corpus Christi

A focus on student success is apparent not only in the support offered to students in trying times but through an increased emphasis on
"early warnings" about student performance in courses and by providing additional academic support to assist students in their studies. This
initiative is telling about President Miller, as her concern for students
has endured since her time as an assistant professor with responsibility
for large classes of first-year students.

Miller has also worked to strengthen the bonds between the local community and the university. The expansion into downtown Corpus Christi, numerous service projects, and a focus on preparing students for careers in the local area all work to benefit the community and students alike. Retaining more of the talented and skilled graduates to support social and economic growth is a shared goal of TAMU-CC and the region. [cxvii]

Bill Nye 'The Science Guy" Lectures in the Performing Arts Center (September 14, 2015)
Texas A&M University-Corpus Christi

Islander Men's Basketball Team (2020)
Texas A&M University-Corpus Christi

Student Life, Traditions, Athletics, and an Odd Mascot

Over its history, the Island University has developed a distinctive culture. Student life is driven through traditions, athletics, events, and symbols that bring the campus together. Each university that has called the Island home has left a mark on the rich student experience enjoyed to day.

Student Life

The Island is home to many different students. Students who enter as freshmen are presented with the opportunity to join numerous organizations, build lifelong friendships, live in a residence hall, and experience a full "traditional" university experience. Other students may attend night classes or take a fully online degree program, with a sharper focus on gaining the knowledge necessary to advance in their careers. These students build professional relationships alongside gaining the knowledge and skills to advance their careers. Still other students enrolled in advanced degree programs may be laser-focused on their pursuit to become experts in their fields and advance the body of knowledge. Put simply, the Island University provides significant opportunity across all levels of higher education from freshman seminars to the awarding of PhDs.

During the years as UCC, there was a significant influence from the BGCT. The curriculum aligned with the ministerial aims of the university as all students were required to take six hours of religious studies regardless of their major or religious affiliation.[cxviii] Student activities at UCC were often reflective of this religious underpinning. The Ministerial Alliance, Volunteer Mission Band, Life Service Band, Baptist Student Union, and other groups all promoted religious ministry and experiences.[cxix] For instance, the Life Service Band performed on-campus religious work in addition to community projects such as weekend trips to conduct youth revivals.[cxx]

Members of the University of Corpus Christi Band (Circa 1950's)
Texas A&M University-Corpus Christi

UCC had several student organizations even in its first year. The 1948 Silver King, the UCC yearbook, listed the Thespians, Engineers, and the Betho Club (for female students interested in home economics) as options for students. Other clubs quickly emerged at UCC including the Art Club, Young Women's Association, Chorus, Band, Pre-Law Club, and the Aggies. The Los Conquestadors were formed to better understand Latin American culture. Clubs were also formed based on the home city of students including Houston, the Rio Grande Valley, and Corpus Christi.[cxxi]

The secular nature of TAMU-CC, as a state-sponsored institution, has changed the student experience to one that is broader and more diverse. Campus life still offers students the opportunity to participate in faith-based organizations such as the Baptist Student Ministry, Young Life, Islander Catholic Organization, and Chi Alpha, a Christian-based student fraternal organization. However, the addition of cultural clubs such as Alpha Kappa Alpha, Black Student Union, India Student Association, Islander Cultural Alliance, Kappa Delta Chi women's fraternity, and the Anime Club highlight the breadth of organizations available to Islanders. Numerous clubs are associated with colleges, departments, and other academic-based pursuits.

Over 150 organizations are available for students to join under the oversight of the University Council of Student Organizations (UCSO). TAMU-CC is a diverse campus with students from many walks of life. A majority of students are women, and many are the first generation in their family to attend college.[cxxii] Often students hold jobs, devote significant time to caring for family members, and may take evening or online courses to better arrange their classes alongside these other obligations.

The student body is formally represented through the Student Government Association (SGA). The SGA President, Vice President, Judiciary, and Senators for each College, as well as other areas (e.g., athletics, housing), are elected annually by students. SGA is guided by their mission statement:

" *The Texas A&M University-Corpus Christi Student Government Association has the dedication and momentum to effectively serve, guide and act on behalf of our student body while promoting the general welfare of our Island Campus.[cxxiiz]* "

Student Government Association Officers (2019)
Texas A&M University-Corpus Christi

Greek life is another important aspect of campus life. In 1960, Kappa Lambda, Tau Delta Delta, and Zeta Chi sororities were founded at UCC. The number of Greek organizations remained relatively stable as some new groups formed and existing groups changed names or dissolved. Following Hurricane Celia, all of the Greek organizations existing at the time, Delta Kappa Psi and Delta Phi Omega sororities, Sigma

Pi, Tau Delta Phi, and Kappa Sigma Kappa, closed within a few years. The closing of the Tau Kappa Epsilon chapter in 1974 would begin a two decade hiatus for Greek life on the Island.

In 1995, Phi Sigma Chi fraternity was founded and marked a new beginning for Greek life. By 2020, International Fraternities with campus chapters included Phi Gamma Delta, Sigma Phi Epsilon, and Sigma Pi. Panhellenic sororities included Alpha Gamma Delta, Gamma Phi Beta, Delta Delta Delta, and Zeta Tau Alpha. The Multicultural Greek Council consists of Alpha Kappa Alpha, Kappa Delta Chi, Sigma Lambda Gamma, and Alpha Phi Alpha. All campus chapters are affiliated with a national organization. These groups regularly participate in community service projects and raising funds for charitable causes at the local and national level. Students involved in Greek life tend to perform better in their courses in addition to the valuable social and leadership skills gained through membership.[cxxiv]

Members of Kappa Sigma Kappa (Circa 1970)
Texas A&M University-Corpus Christi

Sisters of Delta Delta Delta: Emily McDonald, Sarah Pena, Taylor Cope, Jaycie Martinez at Greek Life Meet and Greet Event (2017)
Texas A&M University-Corpus Christi

Traditions

Located near the University Center, the anchor is a focal point for traditions. The first anchor was left on Ward Island by the U.S. Navy after their departure. President Cavness dedicated the anchor to the freshman class and charged the class to maintain the anchor, carry it to sporting events, and guard it against rivals. However, they were not successful in their duties. During a series of pranks with rival universities in the 1960s, the anchor was taken and subsequently disposed of. A new anchor was situated on campus on February 27, 2015 during Homecoming Week. This anchor was placed between the University Center and Science Building in the re-named Anchor Plaza. It is 13 feet long and weighs 5,500 pounds.[cxxv] The original plaque and a new plaque to accompany the second anchor are on display. The anchor is fixed in place to prevent a similar fate as the first anchor.

Members of the Freshman Class Guarding "The Original" Anchor (1950)
Special Collections and Archives, Mary and Jeff Bell Library, Texas A&M University-Corpus Christi

Students Prepare the Anchor for Painting (n.d.)
Texas A&M University-Corpus Christi

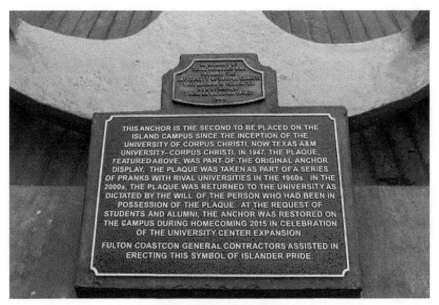

Anchor Plaques (2015)
Texas A&M University-Corpus Christi

Islander Homecoming is held each spring. The naming of a Home-coming king and queen at a home basketball game is the culmination of a week of wide-ranging activities. A pep rally, annual awards ceremony, fiesta, tip-off picnic, pre-game tailgates, and the lighting of the "I" are part of these traditions. The lighting ceremony is marked by the ignition of a large metal structure in the shape of a "capital I" and fueled by propane. Anchors Aweigh is a part of Homecoming Week representing a renewed tradition from the early days of the University of Corpus Christi. This tradition of painting the anchor with a fresh coat of paint was revived in 2018. Service projects have also become part of Home-coming Week with Islander Clean (a time to clean up the campus) and a collection for the food pantry being included.[cxxvi]

Anchor Ceremony (2015)
Texas A&M University-Corpus Christi

Students Participate in the "Lighting of the I" Event (2016)
Texas A&M University-Corpus Christi

During Homecoming, alumni from the Island University are honored at a banquet. Individuals are recognized in three broad groups: Outstanding Alumni, Distinguished Alumni, and Young Alumni. These individuals represent their alma mater exceptionally well as they have excelled in pursuits such as business, the military, academia, professions, or in public service.

Members of the CCSU Alumni Association. John Buckley (Left), Tom Goad (Center), Don Deis (Right)
Alumni Update, December 1982. Special Collections and Archives, Mary and Jeff Bell Library, Texas A&M University-Corpus Christi

Since 2008, Islanders have engaged in an annual BIG Event aimed at providing volunteer service across the community. A similar service day, the Little Event, is held in the fall. The MLK day of service, alternative winter or spring breaks, service Saturdays, and Islander Clean are all regularly-held service events. Students also volunteer in Adopt A-Beach, Strides Against Breast Cancer, Kids Against Hunger, Habitat for Humanity, Grow Local South Texas, Glenoak Therapeutic Riding Center, Volunteer Income Tax Assistance (VITA), Junior Achievement, Mission 911 (homeless assistance), and others.

Students Participating in Volunteer Work (2018)
Texas A&M University-Corpus Christi

The Islander Ring Ceremony is a bi-annual event for junior-level students to be presented with their class ring. This important ceremony is often witnessed by the student's family and friends. Receiving the Islander Ring signifies that you are close to becoming a distinguished member of the Islander Alumni Association and nearing graduation. This is a formal event held in the Performing Arts Center.[cxxvii]

Islander Ring (n.d.)
Texas A&M University-Corpus Christi

Russell Wagner, Director of Alumni Engagement Speaks During the Islander Ring Ceremony. Also Pictured are President Miller, Alumni President Ed Cantu, Vice-President of Student Engagement Dr. Don Albrecht (2017)
Texas A&M University-Corpus Christi

TAMU-CC Student Derrek Arnold during the Islander Ring Ceremony (2018)
Texas A&M University-Corpus Christi

**A TAMU-CC Student Tossing a Sand Dollar in the Lee Plaza
Fountain as Part of the Islander Ring Ceremony (2018)**
Texas A&M University-Corpus Christi

Students Jordan Mayfield and Jeffrey Thomas View Islander Rings in the
University Center (2017)
Texas A&M University-Corpus Christi

Students Ayman Abdalla and Julie
Reyes at Late Night Breakfast (2016)
Texas A&M University-Corpus Christi

Another annual event is Late Night Breakfast held in advance of final exams in December. Students enjoy breakfast in the dining hall as they stay up late to study.

Some places on campus have become traditions in their own right. Dr. Hector P. García Plaza is an outdoor meeting point with a stage and tables to rest or study. Garcia was a tireless advocate for education, stating: "Education is our freedom, and freedom is everybody's business."

Groundbreaking Ceremony for the Dr. Hector P. García Plaza (2005)
Anna M. Canales Photograph Collection of the Creation of the Dr. Hector P García Statue and the Groundbreaking Ceremony for the García Plaza at TAMU-CC, Box 7, Folder 2, Special Collections and Archives, Mary and Jeff Bell Library Texas A&M University-Corpus Christi

The García statue stands nine feet tall and was dedicated in 1996. García was able to view the completed statue in June 1996 just before his passing the following month.[cxxviii] The statue is a point of pride for students who, by tradition, rub the foot of the statue for good luck.

García was a prominent veteran, physician, civil rights leader, and recipient of the Presidential Medal of Freedom. He opened a medical practice in Corpus Christi following his distinguished service in World War II being honorably discharged at the rank of Major. His early community service mostly dealt with public health issues which he addressed through regular radio spots. He would become a noted civil rights leader for his pursuit of rights for Hispanic Americans. He was the founder of the American G.I. Forum, a Congressionally recognized Hispanic Civil Rights Organization.[cxxix]

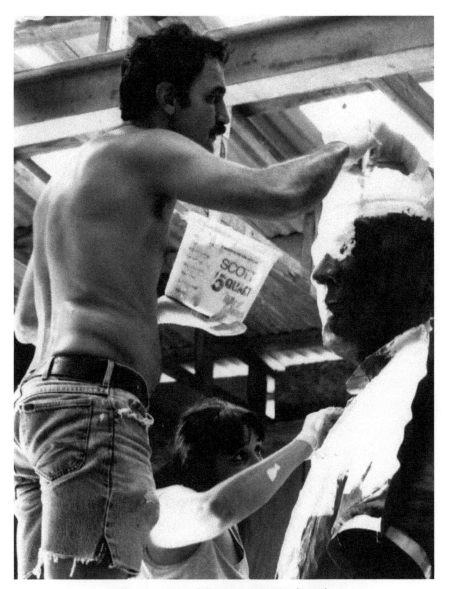

Construction of the García Statue (1996)

Anna M. Canales Photograph Collection of the Creation of the Dr. Hector P García Statue and the Groundbreaking Ceremony for the García Plaza at TAMU-CC, Box 7, Folder 2, Special Collections and Archives, Mary and Jeff Bell Library Texas A&M University-Corpus Christi

Hector P. García Plaza Statue (1996)
*Anna M. Canales Photograph Collection of the Creation of the Dr.
Hector P García Statue and the Groundbreaking Ceremony for the
García Plaza at TAMU-CC, Box 1, Folder 2, Special Collections and
Archives, Mary and Jeff Bell Library. Texas A&M University-Corpus
Christi*

Caliente Television Show Filmed at TAMU-CC for Broadcast
on August 18, 2001 on Univision (2001)
*Special Collections and Archives, Mary and Jeff Bell Library, Texas
A&M University-Corpus Christi*

Captain Hector P. García (Circa 1945)
Dr. Hector P. García Papers, Collection 5, Box 438, Folder 8. Special Collections and Archives, Mary and Jeff Bell Library, Texas A&M University-Corpus Christi

García's work would take many forms, from supporting the desegregation of local schools, resisting the push to declare English as the official language of the United States, improving living conditions in South Texas, and pursuing better labor conditions. He would be appointed to various positions by Presidents Kennedy, Johnson, and Carter. García would be the first U.S. citizen to address the United Nations General Assembly in a language other than English when he gave a speech in Spanish in 1967.

Dr. Hector P. García, Alternative Ambassador to the United Nations (Circa 1967)
Special Collections and Archives, Mary and Jeff Bell Library, Texas A&M University-Corpus Christi

For his work, García received several high honors. Pope John Paul II recognized him with the Pontifical Equestrian Order of Pope Gregory the Great in 1990. President Ronald Reagan would present García with the highest civilian honor, the Presidential Medal of Freedom, in 1984. García was the first Hispanic American to receive the recognition. In 2009, The State of Texas established the third Wednesday of each September as "Dr. Hector P. García Day." President Bill Clinton eulogized him as a national hero.[cxxx]

Near the Garcia Plaza, Cat Alley lies between the Library and the Center for Sciences/Glasscock Center. It is a unique meeting point for students and the many cats who also call the Island home. The i-Cat (Cat Assistance Team) is a committee composed of faculty, staff, and students who care for the feral cats. The team not only feeds and provides medical care for the cats but helps manage the population through a trap-neuter-release program. A student Cat Club also works towards caring for the collective "pets" of the student body.[cxxxi]

iCat on Campus (n.d.)
Texas A&M University-Corpus Christi

Since UCC first took the initiative to make the campus more reflective of the Island environment, this theme has grown to now encompass virtually every aspect of student life. In addition to the naming of buildings in accordance with a nautical theme (e.g., Seabreeze, Tidal Hall, Bayside Parking Garage, Bay Hall) streets (e.g., Oso Lane, Surf Lane, Dolphin Lane, Seagull Lane) and many rooms on campus now reflect this theme (e.g., Anchor Ballroom, the Breakers Break Room, the Cove food court, Seabreeze Patio). Several of the campus parking lots are named for sea animals (e.g., Angel Fish, Starfish, Jelly Fish, Tarpon). Student focused items such as the "SandDollar$" ID Card and S.A.I.L. (online registration portal) further reflect this theme. Names of programs and services often use an "i-" designation meaning "Islander" as a prefix to abbreviated terminology such as with the i-CARE (wellness services), i-News, i-Create (project lab), i-Engage (organization and service portal) among others.

University Mace (n.d.)
Texas A&M University-Corpus Christi

A special time in the life for any student is the commencement ceremony. Wearing a fresh flower lei is a tradition that is unique to Islander alumnus. The lei distinguishes graduates as new members of the Islander Alumni Association.[cxxxii] Other symbols used during the graduation are the university mace and the presidential medallion. The mace is a three-foot-tall wooden emblem that is carried at the front of the processional. The mace is made from wood from one of the old navy barracks on Ward Island and has a medal seal of each of the four universities at its head-UCC, A&I, CCSU, and TAMU-CC. The presidential medal is worn during formal events and has been handed down by each president to the next. This tradition began in 1972 with President Halladay. The Islander Alumni Association promotes traditions and provides the means for over 50,000 alumni to remain connected to the Island University after graduation. The Association has satellite chapters in Houston, Austin, and San Antonio. The Woo Sung Lee Alumni Welcome Center, located just east of campus on Ennis Joslin Drive over looking Oso Bay, is the home of the National Alumni Association. This building was opened in 2010 and named for Lee, an alumni (class of 1959) and businessman, who founded the Boat 'n Net restaurant chain in Texas.[cxxxiii]

Building deep connections is important to students and the university. The Alumni Association uses the slogan "Islander Forever" to signify that alumni are always part of their alma mater. The organization recognizes and welcomes alumni from all four universities to call the Island University home.[cxxxiv]

The Texas A&M-Corpus Christi Foundation shares a similar mission to promote the growth and quality of TAMU-CC. The nonprofit corporation was founded as the Corpus Christi State University Foundation in December 1987. Founding members included Mr. and Mrs. Paul R. Haas, Mrs. John Allen King, Mrs. Margaret R. Turnbull and many other community leaders. By 2020, the Foundation managed $32 million dollars for the benefit of TAMU-CC through scholarships, sponsoring research, endowed chairs and professorships, campus construction projects, and improvements in classroom technology. Notable past trustees include Cecilia Garcia Akers, Linda Benavides, John Buckley, John Chapman, Gloria Hicks, Rosie Mirabal-Garza, Celika Storm, and Karen O'Connor Urban.

TAMU-CC Graduates (August 6, 2016)
Texas A&M University-Corpus Christi

The foundation and university currently manage assets that support 15 endowed chairs and professorships at the Island University.[cxxxv]

- Paul & Mary Haas Endowed Professorship in History
- Conrad Blucher Fund for the Advancement of Science and Technology
- Ennis and Virginia C. Joslin Chair in Accounting
- Rogelio "Roger" Benavides Memorial Chair
- Joe Frantz Professorship in History
- Ruth Campbell Professor of Coastal and Marine Sciences
- Ruth Campbell Professor of Marine Biology
- Harte Research Institute Endowed Chair in Geospatial Sciences
- Harte Research Institute Endowed Chair in Marine Policy and Law
- Harte Research Institute Endowed Chair in Ecosystems and Modeling
- Harte Research Institute Endowed Chair in Fisheries and Ocean Health
- Harte Research Institute Endowed Chair in Socio-Economics
- Miriam Wagenschein Professorship in Women and Gender Studies
- Miriam Wagenschein Professorship in Sociology
- Eve Layman Endowed Professorship in Nursing
- Barbara Silverman Professorship in Literacy
- Margaret and Paul Turnbull Professorship Endowment
- Mary & Jeff Bell Endowed Professorship in Business
- Jessie Frances Neal and Clifton W. Coonrod Endowed Chair in Accounting

Some traditions have not endured to the present. Homecoming Week activities have changed over the years. Past events have included a bonfire as opposed to the lighting of the "I." Perhaps this change can be best reconciled due to a lack of space on the modern TAMU--CC campus as opposed to the smaller footprint occupied by UCC. A snake dance was held as part of pep rallies during Homecoming Week when the Tarpons fielded a football team.[cxxxvi] A homecoming parade was part of the celebration until 1970, being revived again in 2007 and lasting through 2016.[cxxxvii][cxxxviii] The Islander Revue began in 1999 and was held for 18 years ending in 2017. Student organizations performed an eight minute, Broadway-style production in competition with one another. The event was sponsored by the Student Foundation Association.[cxxxix]

Tarpons to Islanders

TAMU-CC Athletics have built strong programs across many sports. As a member of NCAA Division I, Islander Athletes bring national notoriety to the Island University. Attending a sporting event is enjoyable and a source of pride for alumni and the community. Islander Athletes are not only known for their athletic abilities but routinely earn exceptionally high marks in their academic pursuits as well.

Students Attend a Bonfire (Circa 1950s)
Texas A&M University-Corpus Christi

Several athletic programs came and went during the UCC years. It was often difficult to provide the necessary facilities or scholarship support necessary for sports programs. At times, these programs were some of the easiest to cut during financially lean years.

Football was difficult to maintain on the island. The large teams are difficult to recruit and providing the large number of scholarships needed to attract student athletes was a challenge as well. Scholarships were often granted without the financial backing of the BGCT or endowments. This practice placed a burden on UCC to provide education for some student athletes with little revenue to offset the costs. Football facilities are also expensive relative to other sports and require a good deal of maintenance. While the programs may have been unsteady, early yearbooks show a number of events including send-offs of the team to away games and UCC pep rallies held in the chapel.

The first football game ever was a 14-0 loss to the Trinity University Tigers in San Antonio in 1948. Playing mostly against independent and private universities, the team ended the first season with a 3-7 record. In 1950, the team had a very successful 25-1 record. After a two-year hiatus, football returned the campus in 1953 with the construction of a football field on the island.[cxl] However, football would not be included in the athletic program when TAMU-CC brought sports back to the Island University.

University of Corpus Christi Football Team (1948)
Silver King, 1949. Special Collections and Archives, Mary and Jeff Bell Library, Texas A&M University-Corpus Christi

JOE GIBSON
ASSISTANT

WILL WALLS
HEAD COACH

"SMILEY" DAVIS
ATHLETIC DIRECTOR

U.C.C.

TARPONS

1949 SCHEDULE

OPPONENT	DATE		UCC
0	Sept. 10	Ouachita College	24
24	Sept. 17	Trinity University	7
28	Sept. 23	St. Ambrose	16
58	Oct. 1	McMurry College	12
0	Oct. 8	Austin College	14
7	Oct. 15	E. Tex. Teachers College	14
13	Oct. 22	Sul Ross College	0
0	Oct. 29	Daniel Baker College	27
13	Nov. 12	Stephen F. Austin	0
0	Nov. 19	Texas Lutheran College	31
27	Nov. 25	Texas A & I College	12

KICK OFF 8 P.M.

SOUVENIR 25¢ PROGRAM

Buccaneer Stadium

CORPUS CHRISTI, TEXAS

UCC Football Program (1949)
*Silver King, 1950 Special Collections and Archives, Mary and Jeff
Bell Library, Texas A&M University-Corpus Christi*

Other sports such as swimming and boxing were offered at UCC but have not returned to TAMU-CC. UCC had a successful boxing program. One standout, Johnny Cloud, is honored in the Athletics Hall of Honor for his success at the regional and state level in 1956-57. In the same year, Billy Joe Butler competed at the national level. Collectively, the Tarpons won 62 of 78 bouts in team matches in this season.

Johnny Cloud
Special Collections and Archives, Mary and Jeff Bell Library, Texas A&M University-Corpus Christi

The early years of athletics were marked by instability. The high cost team travel often outpaced revenues. There was a high turnover among the coaching staff and some sports would be fielded one year and abruptly canceled before the next season. This occurred with the basketball and baseball teams in 1951. The following year, football was cancelled even after their successful 1950 season. Under President W. A. Miller, athletics would return with a parred-down coaching staff led by Kenneth Robb.[cxli] [cxlii]

UCC completed a field house that was dedicated on November 7, 1968. The building was paid for by the UCC Sustainers Club and Moody Foundation. This building still serves Islander Athletics as of 2021 and is located adjacent to the Dugan Wellness Center. The Sustainer's Club was founded in 1959 by several civic leaders of the Corpus Christi area for the benefit of UCC. In addition to the larger gifts of buildings, the club also assisted with academic items such as faculty research projects.[cxliii]

The Tarpon Club was founded in 1960 as one aspect of Miller's push to re-invigorate athletics while also making them more fiscally sustainable. This group would assist with the costs of the programs by providing items such as equipment.

Bill Joe Butler
Special Collections and Archives, Mary and Jeff Bell Library, Texas A&M University-Corpus Christi

UCC President Maroney was instrumental in obtaining NCAA certification in 1970. Even as this important milestone was achieved, a long hiatus for athletic programs would soon begin on the island. As UCC transitioned to an upper-level public institution under A&I, all sports programs would be discontinued. Athletic programs would began again in 1998 after almost a quarter of a century.[cxliv]

Facilities, teams, and coaching staff would have to be built from the ground up. To lead this effort, Dan Viola was hired in 1997 as athletic director.[cxlv] The community and the Susser family were vital in support for this undertaking. This monumental effort paid dividends as TAMU-CC was accepted as a Division I school in 2002. Islanders compete in 14 men's and women's sports as a member of the Southland Conference. By 2021, women competed in basketball, cross country, golf, soccer, softball, tennis, beach volleyball, volleyball, and track & field. Men's sports were baseball, basketball, cross country, tennis, and track & field.[cxlvi]

Home basketball games are held in the Dugan Wellness Center or in Downtown Corpus Christi at the American Bank Center Arena. Baseball and softball home games are held at facilities located adjacent to the Dugan Wellness Center/Island Hall. Chapman Field is the home of the Islander baseball team and is named after John (1925-2008)[cxlvii] and Louise Ann Chapman (1926-2004).[cxlviii] Occasionally, baseball tournaments are held at Whataburger Field, a minor league ballpark that is home to the Corpus Christi Hooks near Downtown Corpus Christi.

Soccer and track & field are held at the Dugan Family complex on the Momentum Campus.[cxlix] The Thomas J. Henry Tennis Center opened in 2014 as host to the Southland Conference Tennis Championships, with the Islanders winning both the men's and women's titles.[cl] Sand volleyball courts were opened on Momentum Campus in June 2015 as the sport became part of the intercollegiate athletics pro gram in spring 2016. Opened in 2019, the addition of the Islanders Pavilion and Courts at Water's Edge Park provides the team with a bayfront home and serves the Corpus Christi community.[di]

As of 2021, Islander Athletes won 23 Southland Regular Season Titles: Women's Basketball (2020); Women's Tennis (2014, 2016-2018); Volleyball (2015, 2016); Men's Basketball (2007); Women's Cross Country (2007-2009, 2011, 2018); and Men's Tennis (2003, 2008-2015, 2017).[clii]

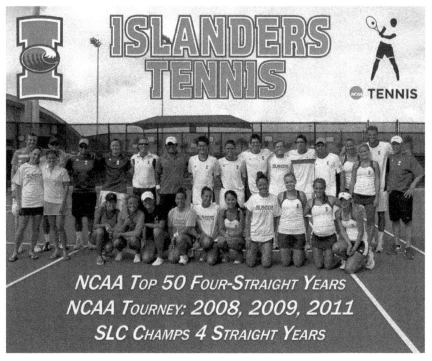

TAMU-CC Tennis Poster (Circa 2011)
Special Collections and Archives, Mary and Jeff Bell Library, Texas A&M University-Corpus Christi

The TAMU-CC Hall of Honor is a recognition for individuals and standout teams who have made significant contributions to TAMU--CC athletics. Teams include the 1971 tennis team which ranked fifth in the nation. The 13 players and coaching staff which comprised the 2004-2005 women's basketball team are honored for their outstanding season and boosting the national prominence of the program. The 2006-2007 men's basketball team was inducted in 2017 based on their 14-2 season with the Southland Conference player of the year, Chris

Daniels (1984-), and coach of the year, Ronnie Arrow (1947-). Arrow would lead the Islanders for eight seasons with a 134-91 overall record. Arrow left TAMU-CC to take the head coach position at South Alabama following the 2007 season.

The 2006-2007 Men's Basketball Team is Inducted into the Athletic Hall of Honor During the Alumni Honors Banquet (2017)
Texas A&M University-Corpus Christi

Among the standout players, Terra Andrews holds the career scoring record with 1,550 points during her basketball career. Standout pitcher Donald "Trey" Hearne (1983-) would play minor league baseball. Tennis star and hall of fame inductee Gonçalo Figueiredo (1981-) would continue to support Islander Athletics as an associate head coach. Hall of Honor individual inductees include Dr. Jack Dugan and President Maroney, among other prominent players, coaches, and supporters.[cliii]

Izzy the Islander

The unique island setting provides for some unusual mascots. TAMU-CC was identified as the "Island University" early in its history and mascots have reflected this trait. The Tarpon, a type of Gulf fish, was the official mascot UCC adopted in 1947. The phrase "eat 'em up Tarpons" served as a rally cry during sporting events.[cliv] Upon the resumption of sports, the Islanders were represented by Tarpie the Tarpon.[clv] There was concern that the Tarpon was poor branding for the university. In particular, the costumed version of the mascot appeared more as a scary bird with blue fur than a fish. Re-branding efforts culminated with Izzy the Islander.

**University of Corpus Christi Students
with a Tarpon (Circa 1940s)**
Texas A&M University-Corpus Christi

Izzy was born on October 13, 2004 as the official mascot complete with a "replacement ceremony" featuring both Izzy and Tarpie.[clvi] In 2011, Izzy received a makeover from the original styling that had included a grass skirt, use of a spear and shield, and a more prominent (and less child-friendly) mask. The revised Izzy has an Islander jersey with board shorts, always sports a "game face," and has a Momentum emblem on the top of a blue and green decorated mask.

Izzy the Islander and TAMU-CC cheerleaders (2018)
Texas A&M University-Corpus Christi

Izzy was envisioned as a combination of influences from a "cool" surfer/beach person, Tarpie the Tarpon, and "a rock-bodied Polynesian from the island of Rapa Nui." Rapa Nui is also known by its European name, Easter Island, a remote Chilean territory most notable for its Moai statues built by the island's first inhabitants. However, the mascot has been a topic of concern over the cultural appropriation of people of Pacific Island descent. Discussions over the use of Izzy as the mascot continue due to a concern over racial insensitivity. Articles in the Islander Waves student newspaper and formal action by the TAMU-CC Faculty Senate have called for Izzy to be replaced or further re-branded. The Island University responded to this issue with forthcoming changes to the mascot.[clvii]

University Spirit

University Slogan: "The Island University"

Colors: Blue (dominate), Green, and Silver (accents)

"

Alma Mater

From the East, From the West, From the North, the South, Alma Mater we praise your name.

As a fire in our hearts none shall ever doubt, That your spirit is kept aflame.

Many people are heard the whole land through, All lifting their voices praising you.

To the ends of the Earth we your worth will hail! Alma Mater our A&M-CC

"

Islander Fight Song

Fight for A and M, A and M C-C Highest Honor, Brave and Strong Ever True will be

Onward to Victory Islanders will Prevail We'll Fight, Fight, Fight Forever A and M C-C!

UCC Alma Mater Sheet Music (Circa 1950s)
Special Collections and Archives, Mary and Jeff Bell Library, Texas A&M University-Corpus Christi

Bright Days Ahead for the Island University

In 1969, Othal Brand (1922-2012) would express disappointment at the loss of UCC as the transfer of the institution to the State of Texas became eminent. The loss of identity and a changed mission could be disheartening especially for the people who worked to build UCC. Moving from a private, religious school to a state-supported institution was a profound shift for the Island University. However, its progression, under several names and leaders, has been impressive.

President Furgason Presides Over the 50th Anniversary of the University (1997)
Texas A&M University-Corpus Christi

At the 50th anniversary celebration in 1997, dignitaries gathered to celebrate its progress. Brand, who went on to serve as mayor of McAllen, Texas, stated at the anniversary, "Now we have realized the dreams of the past. But we never dreamed it would become one of the finest institutions in the nation."[clix] These statements perhaps represent a sentiment for many. The university has been transformed.

While attending the anniversary celebration, Brownie Clapp, the wife of the late UCC President Clapp, noted that she recognized nothing about the campus.[clx] Indeed much has changed. The Island University, as a state school and part of one of the largest university systems in Texas and the U.S., has thrived.

TAMU-CC Campus (2010)
Texas A&M University-Corpus Christi

The Island Today

"   *TAMU-CC Vision Statement*   "

Texas A&M University-Corpus Christi is committed to becoming one of the leading centers of higher education in the Gulf of Mexico region while serving the intellectual, cultural, social, environmental and economic needs of South Texas. As a result, Texas A&M-Corpus Christi will invigorate and strengthen the region and state through its educational programs, research initiatives and outreach efforts.

"   *TAMU-CC Mission Statement*   "

Texas A&M University-Corpus Christi is an expanding, doctoral granting institution committed to preparing graduates for lifelong learning and responsible citizenship in the global community. We are dedicated to excellence in teaching, research, creative activity and service. Our supportive, multicultural learning community provides undergraduate and graduate students with a challenging educational experience through residential, distance learning and international programs. The university's federal designation as a Hispanic Serving Institution (HSI) provides a foundation for closing educational gaps, while its strategic location on the Gulf of Mexico and on the cultural border with Latin America provides a basis for gaining national and international prominence.[clviii]

Fauna of Ward Island (n.d.)
Texas A&M University-Corpus Christi

Fauna of Ward Island (n.d.)
Texas A&M University-Corpus Christi

Little evidence of the Naval Radar Station remains on Ward Island. Some foundations of the buildings can be found in less developed portions of the island. One small warehouse building is still in use that was constructed in 1943. Otherwise, the oldest buildings on campus date to the early 1960s with UCC construction projects.

In 2019, TAMU-CC employed the equivalent of 595 full-time faculty members offering 47 undergraduate degrees, 25 graduate programs, and six doctoral degrees. TAMU-CC holds accreditation from the Southern Association of Colleges and Schools Commission on Colleges (SACSCOC) to award baccalaureate, masters, and doctoral degrees. Additionally, other colleges carry accreditations for specific programs. Programs in the College of Business are accredited by The Association to Advance Collegiate Schools of Business. The designation is held for both the business and accounting programs. The Commission on Collegiate Nursing Education (CCNE) has approved the baccalaureate and master's programs. The Doctor of Nursing Practice program, began in 2015, is pursuing CCNE accreditation. The Clinical Laboratory Science program is accredited by the National Accrediting Agency for

Clinical Laboratory Sciences. Within the College of Science and Engineering, programs in Geographic Information Systems, Computer Science (Systems Programming), Mechanical Engineering, and Mechanical Engineering Technology are accredited by the Accreditation Board for Engineering and Technology, Inc. (ABET).[clxi]

TAMU-CC Students Pedro Galvan (left), Brittney Sauceda, and Tyanna Gold (2017)
Texas A&M University-Corpus Christi

Geographic Information Systems Students near the MOMENTUM Sculpture (2014)
Texas A&M University-Corpus Christi

**TAMU-CC Student Jonathan Blades
Tries on a Pair of Google Glasses at the
iCore Labs (2015)**
Texas A&M University-Corpus Christi

The College of Education holds accreditation through the Council for the Accreditation of Counseling and Related Educational Programs (CACREP) for master's programs in Addiction Counseling, Clinical Mental Health Counseling, School Counseling, and Marriage, Couple and Family Counseling. The Doctor of Philosophy in Counselor Education is also CACREP accredited. Additionally, accreditation for the Athletic Training Education Program is through the Commission on Accreditation of Athletic Training Education (CAATE). The College of Liberal Arts carries accreditation for music programs through the National Association of Schools of Music.[clxii] These accreditations are a testament to the quality of academic programs across all colleges at the university.

TAMU-CC Students Kristie Mcclane and Emerald Perez with 4th Grade Students at the Early Childhood Development Center (2017)
Texas A&M University-Corpus Christi

TAMU-CC Students Look on as Dr. Valeriu Murgulet Presents a Rock Sample (n.d.)
Texas A&M University -Corpus Christi

Professor of Art Louis Katz Addresses Students (2017)
Texas A&M University-Corpus Christi

Programs in healthcare are the largest undergraduate major on campus with 352 students enrolled in fall 2018. This is reflective of the strong demand for healthcare professionals, particularly nurses, in the Coastal Bend. Business majors and biomedical science are also highly popular degree programs.[clxiii]

Students Attend a Psychology Lecture by Ms. Amanda Foy in Bay Hall (2016)
Texas A&M University-Corpus Christi

Graduate education is an important offering for TAMU-CC. A total of 659 master's degrees were awarded in the 2018-2019 academic year. The Master of Business Administration degree was the largest graduate program with 314 degrees awarded. The College of Business also awarded 25 Master of Accountancy (MAcc) degrees. Master's degrees were awarded by every college including 116 by Education, 94 by Nursing and Health Sciences, 57 by Science and Engineering, and 53 by Liberal Arts. TAMU-CC offers doctoral degrees in every college except for Business. The College of Education awards the most degrees at the doctoral level with 28 conferrals in the 2018-2019 academic year.[clxiv]

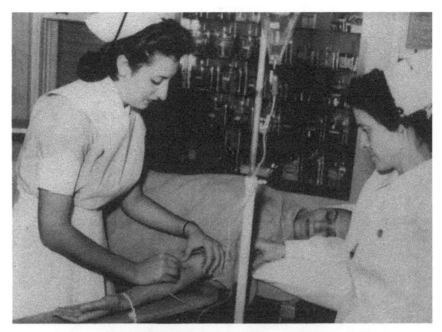

University of Corpus Christi Nursing Students (Circa 1948-1949)
Texas A&M University-Corpus Christi

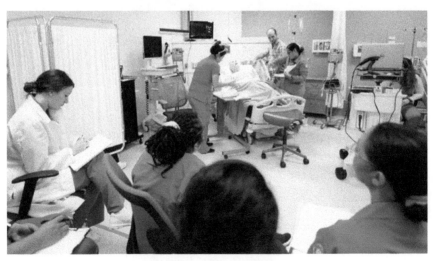

TAMU-CC Students Lorisa Gallardo, Angela Rivera, and Mark Perez Participate in a Clinical Exam (2016)
Texas A&M University-Corpus Christi

The Mary and Jeff Bell Library provides academic support for students and faculty across all colleges. The staff of professional librarians oversee a collection of over 392,000 volumes, extensive online databases with access to over 220,000 eBooks, an i-Create lab (a multipurpose makerspace), numerous technology resources, and study areas. The special collections section of the library houses the Daniel E. Kilgore, Blucher Family Papers, and Dr. Hector P. García papers. The archives houses university records since the founding of UCC in 1947. This collection includes a vast number of photographs, UCC yearbooks from 1948-1973, and other records such as catalogs and alumni magazines.[clxv]

TAMU-CC Students Jackie Roman, Zac Lewis, Vinnie Von Poyveld, and Justin Dear in the Mary and Jeff Bell Library (2017)
Texas A&M University-Corpus Christi

The university continues to impact the community through several centers, programs, and initiatives. The Early Childhood Development Center serves Corpus Christi Independent School District students and provides hands-on training for teachers.[clxvi]

Founded in 1945, the Art Museum of South Texas has been an affiliate of TAMU-CC since 1995.[clxvii] The museum is located on Corpus Christi Bay with views of the ship channel and Harbor Bridge. The current building dates from 1972 and is an impressive post-modern structure designed by renowned architect Phillip Johnson. Among his best-known designs are the modernist Glass House in New Canaan, Connecticut, 550 Madison Avenue in New York City, and 190 South La Salle Street in Chicago. Johnson is also noted for serving as the architect for several other museum projects.

The Miller addition to the museum was completed in 2006 and named for William "Bill" (1926-2007)[clxviii] and Maurine Miller (1927-2021)[clxix] of Corpus Christi. This new wing was designed by renowned architect Ricardo Legorreta (1931-2011) to complement the original structure.[clxx] Legorreta designed numerous buildings in Mexico and the United States including the Camino Real Hotel in Mexico City, Torre BBVA Bancomer tower in Mexico City, the IBM Factory in Guadalajara, the Cathedral of Managua, the San Antonio Public Library, and Children's Discovery Museum of San Jose.[clxxi]

The art museum's permanent collection focuses on regional works but holds works across multiple periods, mediums, and several categories (sculpture, paintings, drawings, and decorative arts). The museum has ample space to host large special exhibits allowing the Coastal Bend to attract exceptional visiting collections.

Art Museum of South Texas Under Construction (1974)
University of North Texas Archives

Gallery of the Art Museum of South Texas (2017)
Texas A&M University-Corpus Christi

Another community outreach location is the Antonio E. Garcia Arts and Education Center located in West Corpus Christi. The center provides programs in arts, health, literacy, and culture to the community. For instance, summer camps are held on writing, ceramics, and mathematics. As an affiliate of the College of Education and Human Development, the center's programming is focused on children and families.[clxxii] Antonio E. Garcia (1901-1997), the namesake of the center, was born in Mexico but was sent to live with family in the U.S. as a safety precaution during the Mexican Revolution. Garcia would spend most of his adult life in Corpus Christi working as a painter and art teacher. His works are reflective of Mexican and Latin culture and several may be viewed as part of the permanent collection of the Art Museum of South Texas and at the Garcia Center.[clxxiii]

TAMU-CC Students Conducting a Health Fair at the Garcia Center (2015)
Texas A&M University-Corpus Christi

The College of Business operates the Coastal Bend Business Innovation Center (CBBIC) housed in the TAMU-CC Flour Bluff Building on South Padre Island Drive. The Center provides entrepreneurs with a range of services to both on and off-site client companies. A focus of the center is to cultivate local businesses to create jobs and positive economic impact.[clxxiv] The CBBIC is designated as part of the U.S. Economic Development Administration's University Center Economic Development Program. Centers in this program work to deploy resources from affiliated universities into communities to encourage economic development.[clxxv] The college also added the South Texas Economic Development Center in 2014. The center produces regional monthly and annual economic reports. Regents Professor Dr. Jim Lee serves as the inaugural director of research for the center.[clxxvi]

The Flour Bluff Building is also home to the Lone Star Unmanned Aerial System Center of Excellence & Innovation (LSUASC). LSUASC is one of only seven Federal Aviation Administration designated centers for unmanned aircraft system research in the U.S. Established in 2013, this center conducts research, development, testing and evaluation of unmanned aerial systems for educational, public, and commercial uses. Clients include public safety agencies, the oil & gas industry, scientific researchers, and government agencies.[clxxvii]

**Lone Star Unmanned Aerial System
(UAS) Vehicle (n.d.)**
Texas A&M University-Corpus Christi

A notable achievement of Lone Star UAS is its partnership with NASA. In 2019, NASA selected LSUASC as one of two test sites to spearhead testing in the Unmanned Aircraft Systems Traffic Management project. The center was chosen for their past work with NASA, expertise in the field, and the challenging environment that the Coastal

Bend represents for operating unmanned aircraft systems. LSUASC and its partnerships provide ample opportunity for TAMU-CC students to be involved in projects as interns and participants in large scale tests. The opportunity to study UAS on such a deep level is only available at a handful of universities.[clxxviii]

Lone Star Unmanned Aerial System (UAS) Command Center
(n.d.)
Texas A&M University-Corpus Christi

Student Access

One of the primary reasons for the state to desire a public university in Corpus Christi was accessibility. TAMU-CC has a high acceptance rate for those who apply. In 2018, 87.1% of prospective students were accepted. Students from 47 of the 50 U.S. states and 176 of the 254 Texas counties attended TAMU-CC in fall 2019. The mission of the university to serve South Texas is evident by the large enrollments from counties in the region. Nueces County (Corpus Christi) has the largest representation of any county at 3,509 students. Other counties with large numbers of their residents attending include Bexar (San Antonio) (819), Harris (Houston) (754), and nearby San Patricio (Sinton) (464).[clxxix]

Another major factor for the desire to bring a state university to Corpus Christi was to address the barrier created by the high tuition cost for attending a private school. In 2018, the tuition and fees for full-time attendance for the year were approximately $9,760. The average amount of educational debt for a TAMU-CC student is $37,454. While this level of student debt rate is not out of line with peer institutions, the amount is the highest among the TAMUS universities located in South Texas. TAMU-CC tuition is higher than other Texas A&M University System universities such as Texas A&M University-San Antonio ($8,245) or Texas A&M University-Kingsville ($8,462). However, it is considerably lower when compared to Texas A&M University-College Station, as their projected cost was $10,316 in 2019.[clxxx]

One reason contributing to higher debt for TAMU-CC students is that a lower percentage of students receive Pell Grants compared to other peer institutions in South Texas. These grants are one of the largest sources of Federal Government Aid and are granted to students with economic need. Among the four A&M universities in South Texas, TAMU-CC had the lowest percentage with 42.2% of students receiving Pell Grants in 2018. Texas A&M International University is the highest with 63.1% of students receiving this type of aid.[clxxxi]

Had UCC not been transferred to the state and continued as a private university, the tuition would undoubtedly be significantly higher. Among the universities that remain affiliated with the BGCT, tuition and fees are closer to $30,000 annually as reported in 2018-2019. For instance, Howard Payne University was $29,198, Mary Hardin Baylor was $29,700, and Baylor University in Waco was $47,364. The least costly BGCT institution was Wayland Baptist at $22,658 per year. Private schools affiliated with other denominations located in San Antonio, the closest geographically to Corpus Christi, are also relatively expensive. Trinity University states an annual tuition and fees rate of $44,600 while University of the Incarnate Word estimates tuition and fee costs at $32,576.[clxxxii] These examples of cost illustrate the concern that private education limits the number of students who are able to attend due to expense.

The cost of attending university has increasingly shifted to students and families as state appropriations for higher education as a percentage of the total cost has decreased over time. However, the importance of pursuing higher education has increased as more careers require bachelors or advanced degrees. In this environment, maintaining accessibility for students often involves financial considerations. This situation further emphasizes the importance of scholarships and other support for educational institutions.

The Future

The unique setting of the island has made for a rich environment. Native vegetation remains in less developed areas of campus, particularly in the southern portion of the island beside the Cayo del Oso. A trail extends around the south side of the island providing for a scenic walk or jog. Extensive and unique non-native landscaping exists near the buildings and pathways of the central campus. Across Ocean Drive from the Performing Arts Center lies a strip of sandy beach. A unique feature near the campus, this additional recreational area connects the campus to Corpus Christi Bay. With more than 223 sunny days a year,[clxxxiii] chances are that classes are being held on a bright day with a breeze off the gulf.

Ward Island (2015)
Texas A&M University-Corpus Christi

A picturesque setting is the stage for the future of the Island University. TAMU-CC is a diverse institution that serves a region with a history shaped by Spain, Mexico, the Republic of Texas, and the US. In the past 75 years, the Island has seen robust change. In 1947, a utilitarian naval training faculty was the start of a transformation into a modern university that is a component of one of the nation's largest systems of higher education. The bond between TAMU-CC and the community is strong having been forged over decades of change and based in mutual need. The institution increasingly engages in globally impactful projects while hosting a sizable community of international students. Each semester hundreds of graduates become "Islanders Forever" and tell the story of the Island University through their own pursuits and success. The Island University has taken several names, been guided by many leaders, and served as home for tens of thousands of Islanders during some of the most formative years of life.

Sunset from TAMU-CC Campus (n.d.)
Texas A&M University-Corpus Christi

References

[i] Palmer, D. (1989, May 27). S. Texans watch as Clements signs education-merger, 4-year CCSU bills. Corpus Christi Caller-Times, p. 1.

[ii] Young, N. B. (2020, August 26). Texas A&M University-Corpus Christi. Texas State Historical Association Handbook of Texas: https://www.tshaonline.org/handbook/entries/texas-a-m-university corpus-christi

[iii] History of the UT System. (2020, August 23). The University of Texas System. https://www.utsystem.edu/offices/chancellor/his tory-ut-system

[iv] About. The Texas A&M University System: https://www.tamus.edu/system/about/

[v] Hunter, C. A., & Hunter, L. G. (2000). Texas A&M University Kingsville. Charleston, SC: Arcadia.

[vi] Palmer, D. (1989, May 27). S. Texans watch as Clements signs education-merger, 4-year CCSU bills. Corpus Christi Caller-Times, p. 1.

[vii] Palmer, D. (1989, May 27). S. Texans watch as Clements signs education-merger, 4-year CCSU bills. Corpus Christi Caller-Times, p. 1.

[viii] History of The University of Texas Rio Grande Valley. (2020, August 30). The University of Texas Rio Grande Valley. https://www.utrgv.edu/en-us/about-utrgv/history/index.htm

[ix] Barry B. Thompson. (2014, March 5). Obituaries. Fort Worth Star Telegram. https://legcy.co/3wKpNAw

[x] Past Chancellors. (2021). The Texas A&M University System. https://chancellor. tamus.edu/ about/past-chancellors/

[xi] Biography. (2021). The Texas A&M University System. https://chancellor. tamus.edu/ about/biography/

[xii] About. (2021). The Texas A&M University System. https://www.tamus.edu/system/about/

[xiii] Young, N. B. (2020, August 26). Texas A&M University-Corpus Christi. Texas State Historical Association Handbook of Texas On

line.https://www.tshaonline.org/handbook/entries/texas-a-m-university-corpus-christi

[xiv] Howard, H. (1998, January 1). A&M-CC gaining funds, teams, buildings, more under Furgason. Corpus Christi Caller-Times.

[xv] Robert R. Furgason. Personal communication to author, June 15, 2021.

[xvi] Halladay, D. W. (1972, December 31). Texas A&I-CC plans to be flexible, original in scope. Corpus Christi Caller-Times, p. 81.

[xvii] Ray, S. (1995, March 15). Big boost for A&M-CC Truan files bills to create a health science center. Corpus Christi Caller-Times, p. 1.

[xviii] Arlington, Texas has a larger population than Corpus Christi and does not have a professional school within the city limits. As part of the Dallas/Fort Worth metroplex, Arlington is located within proximity to multiple professional schools.

[xix] Deselms, J. (1995, May 13). School makes history with doctoral degrees. Corpus Christi Caller-Times.

[xx] Fernandez, I. (2003, October 12). New Harte doctoral program seen as growth spur - It is A&M-CC's first doctoral in science. Corpus Christi Caller-Times, p. 4.

[xxi] Fernandez, I. (2004, April 24). A&M-CC doctorate may help literacy - Program to stress reading instruction. Corpus Christi Caller Times.

[xxii] Dietz, K. (1993, June 1). CCSU, A&I stand to benefit from legislative priorities. Corpus Christi Caller-Times, A5.

[xxiii] Dietz, K. (1993, June 1). CCSU, A&I stand to benefit from legislative priorities. Corpus Christi Caller-Times, A5.

[xxiv] Howard, H. (1998, January 1). A&M-CC gaining funds, teams, buildings, more under Furgason. Corpus Christi Caller-Times.

[xxv] Averty, L. (1996, August 15). Day of firsts - With beaming smiles and streaming tears, a year of change begins for local schools. Corpus Christi Caller-Times.

[xxvi] Mortensen, E. (1993, October 8). Around the city: University expands. Corpus Christi Caller-Times.

[xxvii] Deselms, J. (1995, July 30). A&M Corpus Christi shaping city's growth. Corpus Christi Caller-Times.[xxviii] Howard, H. (1997, October 31). Bush praises local reading efforts. Corpus Christi Caller-Times.

[xxix] Howard, H. (1997, September 4). Work begins on A&M-CC student center. Corpus Christi Caller-Times.

[xxx] Shirley Durrill. (2008, June 16). Obituary. Houston Chronicle. https://www.legacy.com/us/obituaries/houstonchronicle/name/shirley-durrill-obituary?n=shirley-durrill&pid=111659306

[xxxi] William R. Durrill. (2016, April 10). Obituary. Corpus Christi Caller-Times. https://www.legacy.com/us/obituaries/ caller/name/william-durrill-obituary?pid=189557730

[xxxii] Fernandez, S. L. (2003, November 12). New A&M-CC entrance given a warm welcome - Sculpture donated to the university by the Durrills gets good student reviews. Corpus Christi Caller-Times, B1.

[xxxiii] Fernandez, I. (2005, August 26). A&M-CC Bay Hall building near done. Corpus Christi Caller-Times.

[xxxiv] Garcia, K. (2005, April 25). Building at A&M-CC much needed. Corpus Christi Caller-Times.

[xxxv] Day, J. (1998, August 29). A&M-Corpus Christi lands hefty donation. Corpus Christi Caller-Times, p. 1.

[xxxvi] Garcia, K. (2005, April 17). Harte guest of honor at Cliburn concert. Corpus Christi Caller-Times.

[xxxvii] Garcia, K. (2005, April 17). Harte guest of honor at Cliburn concert - Symphony plays first concert in venue he donated to generously. Corpus Christi Caller-Times, B1.

[xxxviii] Performing Arts Center. (2020, August 31). Texas A&M University-Corpus Christi: https://pac.tamucc.edu/

[xxxix] Gordon E. Landreth. (2021). Texas A&M University-College Station. http://www.arch.tamu.edu/community/former-students/outstanding-alumni/2016/g-landreth/index.html

[xl] Dr. J. Christopher Jaffe. (2013, June 5). Obituaries. The Post Star. https://poststar.com/lifestyles/announcements/obituaries/dr-j christopher-jaffe/article_dd8d56de-ce5c-11e2-b000-0019bb2963f4.html

[xli] Performing Arts Center. (2021). https:/ /pac.tamucc.edu/

[xlii] Fernandez, I. (2004, December 10). Furgason recalls campus growth - A&M-CC president credits community for college's success. Corpus Christi Caller-Times.

[xliii] Island University Engineering Building named in Honor of President Emeritus Robert R. Furgason. (2018, December 7). Texas A&M University-Corpus Christi. https://www.tamucc.edu/news/2018/12/furgason-engineering-building-dedication.html#.X0gqd8hK-iUk

[xliv] Jares, A. (2000, September 23). $46 million gift for A&M-CC. Corpus Christi Caller-Times, p. 1.

[xlv] Meighan, T. (2003, April 18). $45M in A&M bonds are OK'd- The money will build facilities here, Kingsville. Corpus Christi Caller Times, A1.

[xlvi] Dietz, K. (1993, June 1). CCSU, A&I stand to benefit from legislative priorities. Corpus Christi Caller-Times, A5.

[xlvii] Tunnell, J. W. (2010). History of the Harte Research Institute for Gulf of Mexico Studies at Texas A&M University-Corpus Christi. Gulf of Mexico Science, 28(1) 56-70.

[xlviii] Tunnell, J. W. (2010). History of the Harte Research Institute for Gulf of Mexico Studies at Texas A&M University-Corpus Christi. Gulf of Mexico Science, 28(1) 56-70.

[xlix] Press Release. (2020, August 13). HRI celebrates Shark Week with Driscoll Children's Hospital. Texas A&M University-Corpus Christi. https:/ /www.harte.org/news/hri-celebrates-shark-week-driscoll-childrens-hospital

[l] Flavius Killebrew, President and CEO of Texas A&M University Corpus Christi, Announces his Retirement at State of the University. (2016, September 14). Texas A&M University-Corpus Christi. https://tamucc.edu/news/2016/09/091416%20Killebrew%20Re tires.html#.X0giR8hKiUm

[li] About Ed Harte. (2020, August 27). Texas A&M University Corpus Christi. https://www.harteresearchinstitute.org/node/217

[lii] Tunnell, J. W (2010). History of the Harte Research Institute for Gulf of Mexico Studies at Texas A&M University-Corpus Christi. Gulf of Mexico Science, 28(1) 56-70.

[liii] Flavius Killebrew, President and CEO of Texas A&M University-Corpus Christi, Announces his Retirement at State of the University. (2016, September 14). Texas A&M University-Corpus Christi. https://tamucc.edu/news/2016/09/091416%20Killebrew0/420Re-tires.h tml#.X0giR8hKiU m

[liv] Garcia, K. (2005, September 8). Killebrew touts his 10-year plan. Corpus Christi Caller-Times, p. 9.

[lv] Saenz, I. (2006, September 14). Expansion on horizon for A&M-CC. Corpus Christi Caller-Times.

[lvi] Flavius Killebrew, President and CEO of Texas A&M University-Corpus Christi, Announces his Retirement at State of the University. (2016, September 14). Texas A&M University-Corpus Christi. https://tamucc.edu/news/2016/09/091416%20Killebrew0/420Re-tires.h tml#.X0giR8hKiU m

[lvii] Alvarado, B. (2016, September 15). Outgoing leader set A&M CC on new path - CEO to retire, college focuses on research. Corpus Christi Caller-Times, p. 1.

[lviii] Garcia, K. (2005, February 4). Killebrew to seek more funds. Corpus Christi Caller-Times.

[lix] Goddard, L. (2009, January 24). Islanders to play even closer to home. Corpus Christi Caller-Times, p. 3.

[lx] Saenz, I. (2007, March 30). A&M-CC fee hike passes by 12 votes - $8 increase will help fund $21M Wellness Center. Corpus Christi Caller-Times. Retrieved from Corpus Christi Caller-Times.

[lxi] Saenz, I. (2007, March 30). A&M-CC fee hike passes by 12 votes - $8 increase will help fund $21M Wellness Center. Corpus Christi Caller-Times.

[lxii] Boscamp, R. (2010, June 30). A&M-CC dedicates new building. Corpus Christi Caller-Times, p. 11.

[lxiii] Saenz, I. (2007, December 17). A&M-CC plans center for alumni. Corpus Christi Caller-Times, p. 3.

[lxiv] Fernandez, I. (2003, October 10). Lee Fountain dedicated - Alumnus Woo Sung Lee gives $300,000 to build plaza at Texas A&M CC. The Corpus Christi Caller-Times.

[lxv] Spangler, S. (2019, April 11). Islander Tribute honors the memory of departed students. Texas A&M University-Corpus Christi. https://www.tamucc.edu/news/2019/04/041119_islander_tribute.html#.X0xn9shKiUk

[lxvi] Nearly 250 Islander students receive their Islander Ring. (2017, November 7). https://www.tamucc.edu/news/2017/11/110717%20Ring%20Ceremony.html#.YNPshflKiUk

[lxvii] Islander Tribute. Texas A&M University-Corpus Christi. https://sga.tamucc.edu/islandertribute.html

[lxviii] Boscamp, R. (2010, September 9). A&M-CC president: Future looks good. Corpus Christi Caller-Times.

[lxix] building's - business - is business. (2009, June 25). Corpus Christi Caller-Times.

[lxx] Preserving History- Creating a Legacy. (n.d.) Christus Spohn Health System Foundation. https://www.christusspohnfoundation.org/ preserving-history-creating-a-legacy/

[lxxi] Michael A. O'Connor (2003, July 25). Obituary. Corpus Christi Caller-Times. https://legcy.co/3vig6kN

[lxxii] Goddard, L. (2011,June 15). Welcome home-A&M-CC un veils new tennis center. Corpus Christi Caller-Times.

[lxxiii] Dr. Jack Dugan. (2020, August 27). Islander Athletics. https://goislanders.com/hof.aspx?hof=3

[lxxiv] Alvarado, B. (2016, April 29). Area A&Ms pursue growth - Regents OK more housing in Corpus Christi. Corpus Christi Caller Times, p. 1.

[lxxv] Texas A&M University-Corpus Christi Begins Second Phase of Construction on Momentum Village Housing. (2016, July 6). Texas A&M University-Corpus Christi: https://tamucc.edu/news/2016/07/070516%20Momentum%20Vil lage%20Phase%20II%20post%20event%20VNR.html#.X0hZT8hK iUk

[lxxvi] Camarillo, V. (2019, October 8). TAMUCC introduces eco friendly waste bins. Corpus Christi Caller-Times, p. 3.

[lxxvii] Marsilio, E. (2014, June 14). Ceremony marks expansion of university's student union. Corpus Christi Caller-Times.

[lxxviii] Alvarado, B. (2018, September 13). A&M-CC sets sights on research status - New $60 million building will help university reach goal. Corpus Christi Caller-Times, p. 5.

[lxxix] Lone Star UAS. (2020, August 27). Texas A&M University Corpus Christi. https:/ /lsuasc.tamucc.edu/about-us/

[lxxx] A milestone to celebrate at A&M-CC. (2017, June 21). Corpus Christi Caller-Times, p. 11.

[lxxxi] Kelly M. Miller, Ph.D. (2020, August 27). Texas A&M University-Corpus Christi. https://www.tamucc.edu/about/president/bio.html

[lxxxii] Kelly Miller. (2021, June 23). Email communication with author.

[lxxxiii] Alvarado, B. (2016, November 11). Regents told union can deliver benefits. Corpus Christi Caller-Times, A3.

[lxxxiv] Watkins, M. (2016, November 16). Legislator, A&M chancellor spar over nixed campus merger talks. The Texas Tribune, p. 1

[lxxxv] TAMU-CC Code Blue. (2020, August 30). Texas A&M University-Corpus Christi. https://www.tamucc.edu/codeblue/code blueweather.html

[lxxxvi] Students make Islander impact, donate over 4,000 volunteer hours during BIG Event. https://www.tamucc.edu/news/2018/04/042018_BIG_Event.html#.YNPmkflKiUk

[lxxxvii] Dr. Clarenda Phillips Announced as A&M-Corpus Christi Provost and Vice President for Academic Affairs. (2018, March 1). Texas A&M University-Corpus Christi. https://tamucc.edu/news/2018/03/030118_Provost_Phillips_Announcement.html#.X0vCOchKiUk

[lxxxviii] Planning and Institutional Research. (2020). Texas A&M University-Corpus Christi. https://pir.tamucc.edu/Internal_Re sources/Data_Center/data_center_index.html

[lxxxix] A milestone to celebrate at A&M-CC. (2017, June 21). Corpus Christi Caller-Times, p. 11.

[xc] Denman, B. (2009, April 8). Sid Smith, African American pioneer, dies. Baptist Press. https://www.baptistpress.com/resource-li brary/ news/sid-smith-african-american-pioneer-dies/

[xci] Lochbaum, P. (1979, April 4). Area colleges discourage foreign students. Corpus Christi Caller, p. 19.

[xcii] Goodwin, B. (1983, July 5). Leach cites need for long-range plan. Corpus Christi Caller, p. 14.

[xciii] Texas Higher Education Coordinating Board. (2020, September 6). 2019 Texas Public Higher Education Almanac. http://report center.highered.texas.gov/agency-publication/almanac/2019-texas-public-higher-education-almanac/

[xciv] Planning and Institutional Research. (2020). Texas A&M University-Corpus Christi. https://pir.tamucc.edu/Internal_Re sources/Data_Center/data_center_index.html

[xcv] A to Z Degree Programs. Texas A&M University-Corpus Christi. https://www.tamucc.edu/academics/ azdegrees.html

[xcvi] Planning and Institutional Research. (2020). Texas A&M University-Corpus Christi. https://pir.tamucc.edu/Internal_Re sources/Data_ Center/data_center_index.html

[xcvii] Camarillo, V. (2019, October 2). TAMUCC achieves research designation, university president says. Corpus Christi Caller Times. https://www.caller.com/story/news/education/2019/10/02/ tamucc-state-university-address-highlights-research-designation/ 3777287002/

[xcviii] Dr. Wes Tunnell named as Fulbright Scholar. (1987, Summer). Alumni Update. Texas A&M University-Corpus Christi Bell Library Archives and Special Collections.

[xcix] Regents Awards. The Texas A&M University System. https://www.tamus.edu/ academic/ awards-recognition/regents awards/

[c] Alvarado, B. (2018, September 13). A&M-CC sets sights on re search status - New $60 million building will help university reach goal. Corpus Christi Caller-Times, p. 5.

[ci] A to Z Degree List. (2021). Texas A&M University-Corpus Christi. https://gradschool.tamucc.edu/ degrees/index.html

[cii] Gregg, T. (2019). RELLIS: Recollections 75 years of learning, leadership, and discovery. College Station: Texas A&M University Press.

[ciii] [ciii] Nelson, J. K., Barton, J. A., Hallmark, J. R., & Hamilton, B. C. (2017). RELLIS: A transformational initiative for collaborative education and research. 2017 ASEE Annual Conference & Exposition. https://peer.asee.org/28795

[civ] Gregg, T. (2019). RELLIS: Recollections 75 years of learning, leadership, and discovery. College Station: Texas A&M University Press.

[cv] Gregg, T. (2019). RELLIS: Recollections 75 years of learning, leadership, and discovery. College Station: Texas A&M University Press

[cvi] Nelson, J. K., Barton, J. A., Hallmark, J. R., & Hamilton, B. C. (2017). RELLIS: A transformational initiative for collaborative ed-

ucation and research. 2017 ASEE Annual Conference & Exposition. https://peer.asee.org/28795

[cvii] Gregg, T. (2019). RELLIS: Recollections 75 years of learning, leadership, and discovery. College Station: Texas A&M University Press.

[cviii] About us. (2020, September 6). Retrieved from The RELLIS campus. https://rellis.tamus.edu/about-us/

[cix] About us. (2020, September 6). Bush Combat Development Complex. https://bcdc.tamus.edu/about-us/

[cx] About us. (2020, September 6). The RELLIS Campus. https://rellis.tamus.edu/about-us/

[cxi] Nelson, J. K., Barton, J. A., Hallmark, J. R., & Hamilton, B. C. (2017). RELLIS: A transformational initiative for collaborative education and research. 2017 ASEE Annual Conference & Exposition. https://peer.asee.org/28795

[cxii] Planning and Institutional Research. (2020). Texas A&M University-Corpus Christi. https:/ /pir.tamucc.edu/Internal_Re sources/Data_ Center/data_center_index.html

[cxiii] Buttler, L. (2019, November 8). Texas A&M University-Corpus Christi Purchases Building in Downtown Corpus Christi. Texas A&M University-Corpus Christi. https://tamucc.edu/news/2019/11/110819-downtown-building-purchase.html#.X0sET8hKiUk

[cxv] Kelly Miller. (2021, June 23). Email communication with author.

[cxvi] Coronavirus Updates. Texas A&M University-Corpus Christi. https://www.tamucc.edu/campus-announcements/coron avirus.html

[cxvii] Kelly M. Miller, PhD. (2021). Texas A&M University-Corpus Christi. https://www.tamucc.edu/about/president/bio.html

[cxviii] Wrotenbery, C. R. (1998). Baptist Island College. Fort Worth, Texas: Eakin Press.

[cxix] University of Corpus Christi plans huge expansion program. (1953,June 7). Dallas Morning News.

[cxx] Baptist General Convention of Texas. (1952). Annual of the Baptist General Convention of Texas.

[cxxi] The Silver King. University of Corpus Christi. Texas A&M University-Corpus Christi Bell Library Archives and Special Collections.

[cxxii] Planning and Institutional Research. (2020). Texas A&M University-Corpus Christi. https://pir.tamucc.edu/Internal_Re sources/Data_ Center/data_center_index.html

[cxxiii] About SGA. Texas A&M University-Corpus Christi. https://sga.tamucc.edu/about.html

[cxxiv] Fraternity & Sorority Life. Texas A&M University-Corpus Christi. http://ucsa.tamucc.edu/FSL/index.html

[cxxv] The Anchor. (2021). Islander Alumni Association. https://www.islanderalumni.org/anchor/

[cxxvi] Celebrate Homecoming 2017 with the Island University! (2017, February 9). Texas A&M University-Corpus Christi. https://www.tamucc.edu/news/2017/02/Homecom-ing°/o202017%20NR.html#.YNDnJflKiUk

[cxxvii] Nearly 250 Islander students receive their Islander Ring. (2017, November 7). https://www.tamucc.edu/news/2017/11/110717%20Ring°/o20Ceremony.html#.YNPshflKiUk

[cxxviii] Garcia-Akers, C. (2016). The inspiring life of Texan Hector P. García. Arcadia Publishing.

[cxxix] Garcia-Akers, C. (2016). The inspiring life of Texan Hector P. García. Arcadia Publishing.

[cxxx] García-Akers, C. (2016). The inspiring life of Texan Hector P. García. Arcadia Publishing.

[cxxxi] The Islander Cat Assistance Team. Texas A&M University Corpus Christi https://tamucc.edu/icat/

[cxxxii] The Islander Lei. Texas A&M University-Corpus Christi. https://www.islanderalumni.org/lei/

[cxxxiii] Woo Sung Lee Alumni Welcome Center. Texas A&M University-Corpus Christi. https://www.islanderalumni.org/alumnicenter/

[cxxxiv] Islander Alumni Association. https://www.islander alumni.org/

[cxxxv] Texas A&M-Corpus Christi Foundation. https://ia.tamucc.edu/ foundation/about.html

[cxxxvi] The Silver King. University of Corpus Christi. Texas A&M University-Corpus Christi Bell Library Archives and Special Collections.

[cxxxvii] Saenz, I. (2007, February 3). Islanders to revive parade tradition - Event shows support before tonight's game vs. Sam Houston State. Corpus Christi Caller-Times, A1.

[cxxxviii] Island University celebrates successful homecoming week. (2016, February 11). Texas A&M University-Corpus Christi. https://tamucc.edu/news/2016/02/020916%20Homecom ing%202016%20Wrap%20.html#.YNDmP_lKiUl

[cxxxix] Student Organizations Rocked the Stage at the 18th Annual 'Islander Revue' (2017, November 15). Texas A&M University Corpus Christi. https://www.tamucc.edu/news/2017/11/ 111517%20Islander%20Revue.html#.YNAF6flKiUk

[cxl] Baptist General Convention of Texas. (1953). Annual of the Baptist General Convention of Texas.

[cxli] Wrotenbery, C. R. (1998). Baptist Island College. Fort Worth, Texas: Eakin Press.

[cxlii] The Silver King. University of Corpus Christi. Texas A&M University-Corpus Christi Bell Library Archives and Special Collections.

[cxliii] Baptist General Convention of Texas. (1959). Annual of the Baptist General Convention of Texas.

[cxliv] Fernandez, I. (2004, December 10). Furgason recalls campus growth - A&M-CC president credits community for college's success. Corpus Christi Caller-Times.

[cxlv] Wellnicki, G. (1997, April 1). A&M-CC Islanders brings aboard new ad Dan Viola signed a two-year contract with a $75,000 annual salary as athletics director. Viola hopes A&M-Corpus Christi can begin fielding some teams during the 1998-99 school year. Corpus Christi Caller-Times, C1.

[cxlvi] Sports. (2021). Texas A&M University-Corpus Christi Athletics. https://goislanders.com/

[cxlvii] John O. Chapman. (2008, May 3). Obituaries. Corpus Christi Caller-Times. https://www.legacy.com/us/obituaries/ caller/ name/john-chapman-obituary?pid=189532634

[cxlviii] Louise Ann Chapman. (2004, May 27). Obituaries. Corpus Christi Caller-Times. https://www.legacy.com/us/obituaries/ caller/ name/louise-chapman-obituary?pid=189519271

[cxlix] Campus Info. Texas A&M University-Corpus Christi Athletics. https://goislanders.com/sports/2016/8/25/campus-info.aspx

[cl] Campus Info. Texas A&M University-Corpus Christi Athletics. https://goislanders.com/sports/2016/8/25/campus-info.aspx

[cli] Campus Info. Texas A&M University-Corpus Christi Athletics. https://goislanders.com/sports/2016/8/25/campus-info.aspx

[clii] Islanders Athletics All-Time. Texas A&M University-Corpus Christi Athletics. https://goislanders.com/sports/2018/ 6/22/department-honors.aspx?id=1471

[cliii] Hall of Honor. Texas A&M University-Corpus Christi Athletics. https:/ /goislanders.com/honors/hall-of-honor

[div] The Silver King. University of Corpus Christi. Texas A&M University-Corpus Christi Bell Library Archives and Special Collections.

[clv] Alvarez, K. (2016, January 26). The History of Izzy the Islander. https://islandwavesnews.com/1380/2016-archive/the-history of-izzy-the-islander/

[clvi] Alvarez, K. (2016, January 26). The History of Izzy the Islander. https://islandwavesnews.com/1380/2016-archive/the-history of-izzy-the-islander/

[clvii] Sowder, C. (2019, February 25). Izzy: a mascot appropriating cultures since 2004. Island Waves. https://islandwavesnews.com/7212/opinion/izzy-a-mascot-appropriating-cultures-since-2004/

[clviii] Vision and Mission. Texas A&M University-Corpus Christi. https://www.tamucc.edu/about/vision.html

[clix] Grant, M. L. (1997, October 19). A&M-CC announces $6 million in gifts. Corpus Christi Caller-Times.

[clx] Howard, H. (1998, April 14). 50 YEARS CELEBRATED, FROM UCC TO A&M-CC Name of college at Ward Island site has often changed during course of half century. Corpus Christi Caller Times, B1.

[clxi] Accreditation. (2021). Texas A&M University-Corpus Christi. https://www.tamucc.edu/about/accreditation.html

[clxii] Accreditation. (2021). Texas A&M University-Corpus Christi. https://www.tamucc.edu/about/accreditation.html

[clxiii] Texas Higher Education Coordinating Board. (2020, September 6). 2019 Texas Public Higher Education Almanac. http://reportcenter.highered.texas.gov/agency-publication/almanac/2019-texas-public-higher-education-almanac/

[clxiv] Planning and Institutional Research. (2020). Texas A&M University-Corpus Christi. https:/ /pir.tamucc.edu/Internal_Resources/Data_ Center/data_center_index.html

[clxv] Facts about Mary and Jeff Bell Library. Texas A&M University Corpus Christi. https://library.tamucc.edu/about/library-facts/

[clxvi] Early Childhood Development Center. Texas A&M University Corpus Christi. https://ecdc.tamucc.edu/

[clxvii] Mission Statement. Art Museum of South Texas. https://www.artmuseumofsouthtexas.org/about/

[clxviii] William Ballou Miller. (2007, January 29). Obituaries. Corpus Christi Caller-Times. https:/ /www.legacy.com/us/obituaries/caller/name/william-miller-obituary?pid=189527179

[clxix] Maureen Mary Becker Miller. (2021, June 19). Obituaries. Corpus Christi Caller-Times. https://www.legacy.com/us/obituaries/thenorthwestern/name/maureen-miller-obituary?pid=199118170

[clxx] Two Artists. One Masterpiece. Art Museum of South Texas. https://www.artmuseumofsouthtexas.org/about/architecture/

[clxxi] Minutillo,]. (2012, January 31). Ricardo Legorreta's Legacy. Architecture+ Design. https://www.architecturaldigest.com/story/architect-ricardo-legorreta-tribute-article

[clxxii] Antonio E. Garcia Arts & Education Center. Texas A&M University-Corpus Christi. https://garciacenter.tamucc.edu/

[clxxiii] Ehrlich, A. (2018, April 26). Don't know who Antonio E. Garcia is? You should. Corpus Christi Caller-Times. https://www.caller.com/story/news/special-reports/building-our-future/throwback/2018/04/25/dont-know-who-antonio-e-garcia-you should/550880002/

[clxxiv] Story. Coastal Bend Business Innovation Center . Texas A&M University-Corpus Christi. https://cbbic.tamucc.edu/story.cfm

[clxxv] University Center Program. U.S. Economic Development Administration. https:/ /www.eda.gov/ programs/university-centers/

[clxxvi] Ramirez, C. (2014, September 4). A&M OKs economic development center. Corpus Christi Caller-Times.

[clxxvii] About Us. Lone Star Unmanned Aircraft System Center of Excellence & Innovation. Texas A&M University-Corpus Christi. https://lsuasc.tamucc.edu/ about-us/

[clxxviii] About Us. Lone Star Unmanned Aircraft System Center of Excellence & Innovation. Texas A&M University-Corpus Christi. https://lsuasc.tamucc.edu/about-us/

[clxxix] Planning and Institutional Research. (2020). Texas A&M University-Corpus Christi. https://pir.tamucc.edu/Internal_Resources/Data _Center/data_center_index.html

[clxxx] Texas Higher Education Coordinating Board. (2020, September 6). 2019 Texas Public Higher Education Almanac. http://re

portcenter.highered.texas.gov/agency-publication/almanac/
2019-texas-public-higher-education-almanac/

[clxxxi] Texas Higher Education Coordinating Board. (2020, September 6). 2019 Texas Public Higher Education Almanac. http://reportcenter.highered.texas.gov/ agency-publication/almanac/
2019-texas-public-higher-education-almanac/

[clxxxii] College Navigator. (2020, September 6). National Center for Education Statistics. https://nces.ed.gov/collegenavigator/

[clxxxiii] The 25 colleges with the best weather. Best Colleges Review. https://www.bestcollegereviews.org/colleges-with-the-best-weather/

About the Author

Dr. Andrew F. Johnson is an Associate Professor in the College of Business at Texas A&M University-Corpus Christi. He holds an undergraduate and master's degrees from Tarleton State University. He earned a PhD in 2015 from the University of Texas at San Antonio and joined the TAMU-CC faculty in fall of that year.

A native of north Texas, he was elected to the Stephenville City Council in 2004 and 2006. Prior to his academic appointment, he served as chief of staff to a member of the Texas House of Representatives from 2013-2015. In this capacity, he worked extensively on local government issues, budgeting, and on legislation concerning higher education.

He is published in academic journals in the areas of corporate political activity, political ideology in organizations, international management, human resources, and several public policy areas. At the Island University he teaches multinational management, principles of management, business strategy, and a graduate course on business, government, and society.

Beginning in 2022, Dr. Johnson will serve as the Associate Dean for Student Success in the College of Business at Texas A&M University-Corpus Christi.

CPSIA information can be obtained
at www.ICGtesting.com
Printed in the USA
JSHW070041140123
36250JS00005B/12